He Came Back For Me
A Journey To Restoration

Andrea Krazeise

For His glory ♡

Andrea Krazeise

with
Maureen Detmer & Maureen Haner

XULON PRESS

He Came Back For Me
A Journey To Restoration
by Andrea Krazeise

Printed in the United States of America

ISBN 978-1-60791-835-6

Front cover image taken by: Tony Warren, Impact Media
   Services
Young girl in the photo is the author at age 2

www.xulonpress.com

"In a day when people are desperate for hope, Andrea's story of reconciliation and restoration proclaims God's constant love in our lives. Her urge to find her biological father mattered to her Heavenly Father because He is the God who cares about our hearts and souls. Spanning decades, this story is written with a sweet transparency that shows God's incredible power to orchestrate international events to bring blessing to her."

Jessica Errico
Author and Executive Director
Central Florida Pregnancy Center
Deltona, Florida

"Andrea Krazeise is the real deal. To know Andrea is to love her and to read her story is to learn more about redemption and the power of a God who 'causes all things to work together for our good.' *He Came Back For Me* reminds me of the power of story and how it is in the telling that God is greater glorified and our faith is grown and strengthened."

Maggie Johnson
Pastor Jeremy Johnson's Wife
Northland, A Church Distributed
Oviedo, Florida

"Andrea's testimony is an inspiring message of hope for all women. It is the Lord's goal to restore all relationships and her story is an example of God's redeeming love."

Jan Doxtater
Women's and Jail Ministry Leader
Orlando, Florida

"Andrea's story is not only intriguing and meaningful, but relevant and applicable. It is a must-read for all of us who have ever wondered, 'How could God use me?' In *He Came Back For Me*, Andrea takes readers on a journey of how God has used the hurts, pains, fears, and frustrations of her life to ultimately prepare her for His work...to be accomplished in His impeccable timing!"

Corin Hughs
Women's Ministry Leader
Safeharbor Christian Church
Sanford, Florida

All the days ordained for me were written in your book
before one of them came to be.
Psalms 139:16

Table of Contents

Dedication

To Dave, my beloved husband and "Knight in Shining Armor." During this journey, you never lost faith in me. I am lucky to be in love with my best friend.

Forever yours, Andrea

To my dear children, David, Daniel, and Kate—this memoir began with you in mind. This woman you call Mom is your greatest cheerleader. I eagerly await the story He is writing in your lives.

All my love, Mom

Preface

Me…write a book? That's exactly what I thought. But often friends have tried to persuade me to at least consider it. It always seemed so vain to me. I mean, what was so great about my life that deemed it being book-bound and what would cause complete strangers to rush out and spend their hard-earned lunch money to read it?

Then one day it dawned on me. No one ever thinks her own life story is that interesting. We're interested in other people's lives, not our own. Then I got to thinking, if I were reading my story from an outsider's perspective, truthfully, I would find it quite amazing. My life is no ordinary life, and neither is yours. It's not an amazing story because it's about me. It's amazing because God wrote my life story. Long before He created the world, He knew me and the plans He had for me. That's what's so amazing!

And though this story is about me, it's really not about me. It's about God! It's about how He can make all things new, because only God can take the messes in our lives and use them for His glory. He gives purpose to a life once fruitless and bland, filling it with passion and purpose. He's in the business of restoring lives and turning ashes into beauty. He can mend broken hearts and restore a ruined relationship between a mother and daughter. He can lead a girl to another continent to meet a father she never knew. And only God can fill a man's heart with enough love to raise another man's child as his own.

He can pour His liquid fire into a cold heart and make a joyful servant out of it. He can also ignite a fire in your heart and help you see and do things you never imagined possible. He has a mission for you—something that you were born to do. God also has the amazing ability to restore the years of your life that the enemy has stolen, just as He did mine.

I invite you into my story and hope you will see the awesome power and the incredible love that our God lavishes on His children.

Andrea Krazeise

Chapter One

Into the Unknown

My heart pounded with excitement as the plane pulled away from the gate at Orlando International Airport. I adjusted my seatbelt and looked over at my seven-year-old daughter, Kate. It was her first plane ride and I could see the growing anticipation in her big blue eyes. My husband, Dave, leaned his head back against the seat as the late afternoon sun streamed through the long row of windows. Standing a few feet in front of me, the flight attendant went over safety procedures to prepare us in the event of an emergency. Entertained by her well-rehearsed safety motions, I recall thinking a plane crash or terrorist attack was the least of my worries.

I had been anxiously awaiting this trip for over a year. Actually, in a sense I felt like I had been waiting my whole life to make this journey. I wondered if anything would be the same for me afterward. Looking around the cabin of the plane, a thought occurred to me, *did anyone here know what a momentous event this was for me? Maybe they did and they came along for the ride to cheer me on.*

Dave looked at me with a big grin. I was so happy that my husband and soul mate of 24 years was by my side. As Kate adjusted the volume of her headphones, I thought of our two boys back at home. Our oldest son, David, who was starting his third year of college, couldn't make the trip because of his summer internship program at the University of Central Florida. Our 12-year-old son, Daniel, pleaded for us to let him spend two weeks with his best friend rather than get his cheeks pinched by strangers or (heaven forbid!) have to eat food that didn't resemble chicken nuggets and fries. My little Kate has always been the adventurous type, so she didn't give the trip a second thought.

We were scheduled to arrive in Germany in about 12 hours. Our first stop would be my hometown of Ulm. After four days in Germany we would head by car to Italy, which was our main destination. As excited as I was about it, my emotions vacillated like a ping-pong ball. At every opportunity, my mind would play the "what if" game. *"What if they don't like me? What if I don't fit in? What if they don't accept me and all this falls apart before my eyes? What will I do then? What if this was really a dumb idea?"*

I glanced down at a picture I held of the family that I was planning to meet in a few days. A distinguished and quiet-looking Italian man stood gazing back at me. Standing next to him were his wife and his three grown daughters. They made a lovely family. Being the outsider, would they ever truly accept me? Soon I would see the expressions on their faces, hear the sound of their voices and feel the touch of their embraces. Soon all the "what if's" would be over and I would know.

As we reached cruising altitude, the flight attendants were bustling around making sure everyone was fed and comfortable for the long flight. I closed my eyes and thought about what led me to this moment. The Scriptures say that God knew me before the world began. As I sat there, I wondered, did God really know before He created the world that on June 26, 2007, I would be seated on Flight 932 soaring across the

Atlantic Ocean to attend a reunion that took a lifetime to unfold?

I wasn't sure where all of this was going to lead, but I knew I had to trust that God had everything under control. Even so, the uncertainty of the unknown can test us and challenge our faith. In some ways, the fear and doubt I was feeling was a good thing, for it required me to stay close to God and totally depend on Him.

I was extremely grateful for what God had done to bring me to this point. Looking back, I see the amazing tapestry of people *and* experiences He had woven out of what I thought were just random events and facts of my life. I can see now how even the hardships of my life were an essential part of the fabric. Even the people that crossed my life's path were being used to shape the person I would become. It was as if God had been working to weave each thread right from the very beginning in order to show me that everything I had experienced mattered and that nothing was by accident.

The initial threads of my life were woven in a small town in Germany. That's where my story began, but first I have to tell you about my mother because she is the reason I'm here. Many people make up the tapestry of my life but my mother is the most significant thread.

Post-War Beginnings

My mother, Erica Maria, grew up in the aftermath of World War II. Her mother (whom I will refer to as "Oma," which means *grandmother* in German) and her three children (my mother and her two younger brothers, Jonas and Romas) came to Germany from Lithuania in 1946 as displaced people because of the war. Oma's husband had died fighting in WWII, leaving her to care for their three small children on her own. Displaced citizens during that time were put in DP camps, which today we call refugee camps.

There were hundreds of those camps in Germany and Austria after WWII and they housed over time somewhere between 11 million and 20 million people. The German government operated the camps and charitable organizations such as the Red Cross stepped in to provide humanitarian relief. Even with the humanitarian aid, conditions were harsh. Food was scarce and many people suffered from malnutrition. Sanitary conditions were poor and illness and disease were rampant. Many people turned to alcohol to cope, which led to many other abuses and social problems.

My mother spent her entire childhood years in DP camps. She also spent a lot of time in hospitals because she was underweight and seemed to catch everything that went around—whether diphtheria or some other communicable illness. Fear pervaded my mother's life, especially during her childhood. She remembers seeing the bombed remnants of buildings everywhere, or "broken houses" as she called them. She overheard adults talk about Hitler, the war and how their relatives or neighbors "just disappeared." She had a stepfather for a short time, and then he "disappeared." She was afraid her mother might be next. She was too young at the time to understand that the war had ended, Hitler was dead, and what she was seeing and hearing people talk about was post-war.

The government moved my mother's family from camp to camp. The camps were packed with people from Lithuania, Poland, Russia and other surrounding nations, mostly women and children. My mother told me how Oma once worked in a local ammunition factory when Mother was a baby. In order to work, Oma had to leave my mother in the care of another camp resident. One time the air raid sirens went off and in her haste and confusion, the woman caring for my mother left her lying out in the sun alone while she took cover in a bunker. Oma came home from work and found the caretaker crying hysterically next to an empty stroller.

In all the chaos of the air raid, she didn't know what happened to my mother and tried to explain to Oma. My grandmother, of course, was frantic. Moments later, an Italian man ran up to Oma urgently saying, *"Bambina! Bambina! Per favore, seguirme!"* Oma did not understand what he was saying, but he was motioning excitedly for her to follow him as he imitated cradling a baby in his arms. Oma anxiously followed him to his apartment and once inside, found my mother safe in the arms of the Italian man's wife. Fortunately, they saw Oma around the camp with her baby and knew to whom she belonged.

The final DP camp they were moved to was in Ulm, Germany. The Ulm camp was a collection of long barracks-type housing with ten units in each building. Each apartment contained two very small rooms—a bedroom where the entire family slept and a kitchen/living space, which held a couch, a table with four chairs, a hutch and a stove. There was no indoor plumbing but there was a separate building across the camp for washing clothes and another building that contained outhouses, where once a month, showers and baths were made available.

Each family had to haul their own water to use for daily washing and cooking. Hard work filled their days just for the simple comforts of a hot meal and warm bed each night. Oma, my mother, her two brothers and their dog often took long walks to the nearby woods. It was essential to bring a bucket with them, as they were always collecting either wood for their stove or food. Everyone did their part, including the dog. No one knows why, but he collected rocks.

The government gave each family in the DP camp a small plot of land behind their building to grow some vegetables. Oma's garden grew potatoes, cabbage, sweet peas, and rhubarb, plus a few other vegetables. Sometimes they would go into the fields and pick blueberries or mushrooms. Meat was harder to come by so they did not have it often—except when Oma would get the opportunity to work on a farm. Then they would have an occasional chicken or rabbit.

At one time, a Ukrainian family lived next door. They had a pet chicken named Stanislov who ran loose all over the camp. Once, Oma longed to have something with more substance than potatoes for dinner. Sadly for Stanislov, times were desperate and Oma had watched him cluck and peck around the camp one too many days. The next Sunday, Oma and her three children sat down to a feast—and I probably don't have to mention who the guest of honor was.

Sunday meals like that did not happen too often, but alcohol was always present. Alcohol played a big part in my mother's home life. Oma knew how to make her own wine from strawberries or most any kind of berry. There also was a bar at one end of the camp. Oma turned to alcohol frequently—*and men*—to ease the pain and loneliness of her post-war, single-parent life. She always had a new boyfriend in her life and that meant a new guest in their already cramped quarters. A curtain on a string divided the bedroom for privacy. Every new boyfriend meant a new round of drunkenness, yelling, and fighting to contend with in their home. Because of the many men in and out of Oma's life, her reputation became the talk of the camp.

Oma was miserable. She was a slim woman who rarely smiled at her children. Her facial features revealed hard lines of stress and sadness. Many times she would lean on her young children for the comfort she desperately needed, but regrettably, her children never had the luxury of leaning on her to ease their distress. If my mom cried tears of sadness, she was more likely to see the hand of punishment than arms of consolation from Oma.

Mother herself began drinking at a very young age. When Mom was four years old, she got drunk at one of her baby brothers' baptism service and liked the attention she got from doing that. There were also times when Mother wanted to escape from the unhappiness and despair that surrounded her. She would go out to a nearby field of daisies and lie in the field, look up at the sky with the flowers above her head and pretend that she was a princess. She didn't know anything else, but even as a child, she dreamed of having a different life. I share these accounts of my mother's younger years to give you some insight into the emotional impact it had on her and how it would ultimately impact my life, like a generational curse.

Agents from child services often visited Oma. The agency determined removing the children from Oma's custody would be in their best interest. Therefore, when Mother was ten years old, they sent her to a Catholic girl's school at a convent an hour away from Ulm. They sent her two younger brothers, Jonas and Romas, to a Catholic monastery for boys in Italy. Oma explained to her children that the move would only be temporary and it would allow Oma to find a good job. She assured them they would be back with her within a few months.

Those few months turned into six years. On the day that Mother was to leave for the convent, Oma packed her daughter's suitcase and promised to visit her every Sunday. Mother clung to those words and every Sunday for six years she would stand by the front gate waiting and watching for Oma. As every bus stopped, she thought for certain Oma would step off, but each time the doors closed, my mother's heart sank with disappointment. Oma never visited her daughter in the six years she was away. During that time, Mom only received five letters from Oma. My mother was heartbroken and that experience left her with strong feelings of abandonment and rejection. Those emotions would affect my mother's life for years to come.

At age 16, Mother finished school at the convent and returned to Ulm. Oma was still living in a DP camp and Mother refused to go back there, so she got a job at a daycare operated by nuns and lived upstairs above the nursery. She visited Oma in the DP camp on occasion and eventually Oma was approved for a government-subsidized apartment. After a few months at the daycare, Mother took a position at the same factory that Oma worked at making electric blankets. Before long, Mother and her two brothers, who had returned from Italy, were all living with Oma in the new apartment.

Living with Oma again was no treat for Mother. Oma made it very clear that my mom would have to be responsible for herself, including anything she needed or wanted to buy. That seemed to be okay with Mother because by then she was 17 and used to looking out for herself. With a full-time job and lots of friends, it was easy to find entertainment after work and avoid going home to Oma. Mother would frequently stop at a restaurant or a pub on her way home from work for a beer. Sometimes she went with one of her brothers, sometimes with friends, and sometimes she went alone. Mother was underage, but that didn't seem to be a problem.

One particular evening, Mother stopped by a local Italian restaurant called Bella Napoli for a drink. While sitting at the bar drinking a glass of beer, she noticed a handsome young Italian man waiting tables. Mother had already had several boyfriends in her life, but none had lasted. Sitting there with the familiar ache of loneliness, she became aware of the beautiful Italian music that filled the air and of the waiter's flirtatious smile. A few days later, Mother went back to Bella Napoli hoping the same waiter would be there. He was working that night and she learned his name was Giulio. She found that, even though he was Italian, he could speak a little German—at least enough to converse with a pretty teenager. Giulio and my mother hit it off and within weeks began dating.

Mother's heart began to come alive with hopes and dreams of a future with Giulio, especially once he told her all the things her heart longed to hear. After Giulio's shifts at the restaurant, they would take long romantic walks along the Danube River and stroll through the town of Ulm to window shop. The beautiful window displays would change every few weeks, capturing Mother's imagination and the dreams of having a normal, happy life with a husband, a home and children—unlike the environment she grew up in. Giulio professed his love to my mother and it was not long before their relationship turned intimate. Mother felt loved and cherished and wanted by Giulio.

Within a year, during a visit to her doctor, Mother learned that she was pregnant with me. Elated with the thought that this was going to be the start of her happy future, she ran as fast as she could to the restaurant where she breathlessly exclaimed to Giulio, "I'm pregnant!"

Giulio's jaw dropped when he heard the news. His face said it all—he was in shock. The last thing in the world he wanted was to be a father. He told her that he wanted nothing more to do with her from that moment on. His reaction instantly doused the flame of their young love. In just a matter of minutes, her hopes and dreams came crashing down around her. In disbelief of Giulio's unexpected response, my mother left the restaurant numb and confused. How could a man who claimed to love her, who made plans for their future, reject and hurt her like that? In the darkness of the night, she walked home with her two familiar companions— rejection and abandonment. It seemed like a cruel joke the world was playing on her.

Had Abortion Been Legal

No one sang over me as I grew inside my mother's womb. No one prayed over me and no one joyfully talked about my upcoming entrance into the world. Everyone was angry for one reason or another. Mother was hurt and wounded. What should have been a blessed event was a constant reminder of the pain and rejection my mother felt. My existence complicated things for Mother. There she was pregnant with a child that even the father didn't want. Then there was Oma, who was very controlling, and with their relationship already strained, she couldn't even *think* of telling Oma she was pregnant with me. In truth, Mother was afraid of Oma. Living in the government projects didn't help matters, as the last thing they needed was another mouth to feed. Mother just wanted me, or "*it*" to go away. Because of me, her dreams had been crushed. If abortion had been legal in 1963, that would have been my fate.

As I now reflect and imagine the anguish and despair my mother must have gone through while carrying me, I thank God when I read Psalms 139 where it says, *"My frame was not hidden from you when I was made in the secret place. When I was woven together in the depths of the earth, your eyes saw my unformed body. All the days ordained for me were written in your book before one of them came to be."* With all the turmoil that surrounded my mother, God still had my life in His hands. He saw my tiny frame inside her womb and knew all the days that were ahead of me before I was even born. In fact, my days were written in His book before they came to be. God had a plan for me, even in the midst of that crisis pregnancy.

Mother kept quiet about the pregnancy as long as she could. In fact, it was months before Oma discovered her secret. This is how it happened. One day Oma came home and began telling Mother about a co-worker who just found out about her own pregnancy. *"Good for her,"* Mother thought sarcastically to herself as she stood at the sink washing dishes in silence, not wanting to take part in Oma's conversation. A few weeks passed. Oma came home and once again began talking to my mother about yet another woman who just found out she was pregnant. That time Mother took the bait, turned around and said, "Me, too!" and without missing a beat, turned back to the sink and continued her chore.

Oma unleashed her fury. "I knew it!" she shouted, "Well, don't expect any help from me! You've made this mess, now you have to deal with it!" Oma's tirade went on and on for days. My mother cried for weeks, realizing she had no one to count on for support, either financially or emotionally.

By the time she was in her sixth month of pregnancy, Mother quit her job at the electric blanket factory and got another job at a paper factory. That change of jobs must have been God-directed because it was the saving grace for both of us. At the new factory Mother met two older Ukrainian women with hearts of compassion. As Mother's waistline grew, those two women took her under their wings and showed her the love and support that wasn't in the offering from Oma.

The Ukrainian women invited Mother over for dinner and had long talks with her. Along with a hot meal, they gave her lots of encouragement and shared the things to expect while she was pregnant. They gave her little gifts for the baby and became my mother's main lifeline of support. Then the day came when Mother felt me kicking inside of her womb and that little movement of life helped to lift some of her sadness. At last, she thought, *"I'll have somebody to love."*

As the months passed, the time came for her to give birth to me. Her water broke in the middle of the night. She cried out for Oma, "I'm wetting the bed and can't make it stop!" Oma shouted for Jonas to call for an ambulance. Within an hour, Mother was in the hospital delivery room enduring a long and grueling labor alone. By God's grace, I found my way into the world on May 24, 1963 by breech delivery. I weighed in at six pounds, four ounces and was given the name Andrea Dagmar. Confused and in intense pain, Mother did not greet me with a kiss or joyful embrace. Seeing a newborn for the first time came as a surprise to her, as she did not know babies came into the world all slimy and wet.

After several days in the hospital, Mom and I arrived home to somewhat of a surprise. On the table next to my mother's bed sat a vase of red roses left by Oma. Mother laid me down on the bed and sank down beside me. She looked at her tiny helpless infant lying there and, being no more than a child herself, began to weep. She felt overwhelmed with the idea of being a mother and doing it alone. Scared and unsure, floods of tears streamed down her face as she cried out, "What in the world am I supposed to do with this baby?"

Chapter Two

A New Kind of Love

M y mom's life with a newborn was not full of the
"oohs" and "aahs" that usually accompany a joyful
arrival. She was very sad most of the time, probably from
post-partum depression. Added to the new responsibility of
taking care of an infant, she had to do it under the critical,
watchful eyes of my grandmother. The sounds and activity
of a newborn filled their cramped apartment. The 2:00 a.m.
feedings and interrupted sleep were an adjustment for the
whole family. My Uncle Romas was 15 years old, Uncle
Jonas was 13 and the two of them shared a bedroom. Mom
and I shared the other bedroom, while Oma slept on the
couch. Within a couple of weeks, Mom could see some relief
as everyone in the family pitched in to help care for me.
Sometimes, my young uncles would feed and play with their
baby niece when they were not at school during the day.

Those first six weeks, Mom and I were home alone during
the day. While her brothers were in school and Oma worked
at the factory, Mom had time to become more comfortable
with her new role as a mother and bond with me. As her
confidence grew, the day she would have to return to work
fast approached. By the time I was six weeks old, Mom went
back to work and placed me in daycare. Those first days were

extremely tearful for Mom as she watched the factory's clock and counted the minutes until she could take me home.

Eventually, Oma's heart softened toward me and she asked Mom if she could feed me and change my diapers. Oma especially enjoyed giving me a bath. Then what started as a helping hand gradually became "The Takeover," which left my mother feeling very resentful, as if she wasn't good enough as a mother. On the positive side, Oma seemed to go through a true transformation as she became a loving and kind grandmother doting over her new granddaughter. The bright side for my mother was that she had a willing baby-sitter freeing her up to go out at night with friends like she used to. It wasn't long before Oma formed a special bond with me and then she would actually encourage Mother to get out and enjoy some free time.

After a few months, Mom and her friends began going out often and they got acquainted with some of the U.S. servicemen stationed in the area. Many G.I.'s would ask Mom for a date, but she always turned them down, her heart still scarred from the heartbreak of Giulio, and Mom had me to consider as well.

When I was approximately a year old, a tall, handsome G.I. with a shy smile joined Mom's group of friends. His name was Don and he was different from the others. So many of the American soldiers were loud and obnoxious, but Don was reserved and polite. He was also smart and learned early on how that feisty German gal had turned down date after date with his friends. The last thing he wanted was to be another casualty, so he kept to himself. But Don stood out from the crowd and eventually stepped into my mother's heart. Finally, Mom was so bold, she walked right up to Don and asked him out for a date and he accepted.

Once again, there were language barriers. Don did not speak much German and Mom did not speak English. They were never far from an English/German dictionary, though, with both of them trying their best to learn the other's language. Their evenings were spent looking up words from English to German and German to English in addition to movies, dancing and hanging out with friends. Mother explained to Don on their first date that she had a one-year-old baby at home. That didn't seem to matter to him because he continued to see her.

After a month of dating, the day came when Don met me. According to my mother, he was gentle and tender with me and his eyes seemed to light up whenever I was in his arms. One cold Saturday night Don came over, and the three of us sat watching the fire in the fireplace. I was happily sucking my pacifier when Don gently reached over and took the pacifier out of my mouth and threw it into the fire. We all just sat there watching it melt in the flames. Mom froze with fear knowing all the stores had closed by that time of night and she couldn't imagine how I would ever get to sleep without it. As it turned out, I never cried or uttered a peep or ever asked for another pacifier. Don had such a relaxed nature and possessed the instincts of a well-seasoned father.

As Don's visits to our apartment became more frequent, I would run to him and climb up to stand on the top of his feet. He would dance me around the room, picking me up and holding me in a way that made me feel safe and secure. Don was not only falling in love with my mother—he was falling for me, too. And Oma, who let the world know that the sun, moon, and stars rose on her granddaughter, was also open and honest about her feelings for Don. Oma loved Don and told my mother when she first met him, "You're going to marry him!" I'm sure that was music to my mother's ears.

Oma had softened around the edges and seemed more personable than before. My mother struggled inwardly with Oma's new behavior, especially since she had never been the recipient of Oma's affection while growing up. But whatever had happened to my grandmother was a welcome change and it affected everyone in the family. The once harsh matriarch went out of her way to care for me and to show kindness to Don. One time Oma cleaned the house from top to bottom getting it ready for Don to come over for Christmas. Because Oma wanted everything perfectly neat and didn't want to mess up anything for the man that she was convinced would one day marry her daughter, Oma slept on the floor (instead of the couch where she normally slept) the night before his arrival.

The Great Escape

By the time I was three years old, I had a baby sister, Donna. Don and my mother were engaged to be married when Don's military enlistment ended. Don was eager to take his fiancé and two little girls to America. Unfortunately, a problem arose in which Mom didn't have her birth certificate, causing a delay in obtaining her passport paperwork. Mom, Donna and I were unable to leave Germany with Don. He had to return to the States without us.

Though we stayed behind in Germany, Mother didn't feel abandoned. Mom and Don loved each other and she believed he would make a way for her to come to America once her papers were in order. By early spring, Mom notified Don on a Saturday that she was ready to join him in America. Two days later, she received his wire transfer of funds and purchased our airline tickets. By Wednesday Mom had the tickets in hand and on Friday she arrived at the Frankfurt airport with her two little daughters and two suitcases. I was almost four years old and Donna was ten months old.

Mom was overjoyed. She couldn't wait to leave Germany and the pain of her past behind her and move on to a better life. Oma, on the other hand, was tearful and found it difficult to say goodbye, especially to me. I had won my grandmother's heart and now was being torn away from her. Oma anguished with the sad reality that she may never see us again.

Oma made the two-hour taxi ride with us to the airport. While we were waiting at the airport to board our plane, Mom and Oma were saying their final good-byes. As a token of her love, Oma reached into her coat pocket and pulled out two items—a spoon and a wooden cross—and placed them in my mother's hand. Oma explained to her daughter that long ago, when Oma herself was a young woman, she had worked at one of Hitler's factories. Hitler insisted that everyone who worked for him be dressed appropriately— flawless and immaculate.

Oma's skirt was tight-fitting and it had unraveled at the seams. She had fixed it several times, but finally the fabric was beyond repair. One day Hitler was inspecting his factory and Oma, trying desperately to fade into the wall, could not escape his notice. "Get her a new skirt!" Hitler shouted at the guards as he passed by her. Another time, she had forgotten her spoon and was using her hands to eat her lunch. Hitler would have found these manners appalling and unaccept- able. Quickly one of the guards stepped in and gave a tearful Oma his spoon. Two infractions with Hitler could have been disastrous!

After that Oma went to talk with a priest and she shared her fears with him. Even though she was grateful for getting a new skirt and spoon, she was very fearful of what could happen to her. The priest tried to give her some peace of mind so he gave her a wooden cross to hang over her door for protection. It was to remind her that God was watching over her and that He would hear and answer her prayers. Oma had taken the cross down from her wall to give to her daughter as she left for a new life in a new world. That cross still hangs above the entry door in my mother's home.

From a four-year-old's perspective, the trip to America was an amazing adventure. I ran up and down the aisles of the airplane and got handouts of food and candy from everyone. While Donna cried and fussed all the way from Germany to the United States, I ate more treats and sweets than my little belly could contain. Then I spent the rest of the night sick to my stomach.

Mother was so eager to get out of Germany that it really didn't matter what was going on. She was ready to close that chapter of her life; she had no regrets when the plane lifted off the ground and took her away. Mom always thought the Germans had never really accepted the displaced refugees. Because of her thick Lithuanian accent, she had always felt like an outsider. There was no love lost when Germany faded in the distance behind her. This young 20-year-old woman with two children in tow was eager to start a new life.

After a layover in New York, we stepped off the plane in Orlando, Florida. It was a warm spring day in April. Mom was eagerly expecting to see Don waiting for us, but he wasn't there. Mom just stood there, dressed in her heavy winter clothing, with Donna in her arms and me at her side. She didn't know what to do. Finally she managed to ask a cab driver how much it would cost to drive us to Don's hometown of Sanford. "That'll be 20 dollars," he said. That was the exact amount of money Mom had.

As we were piling into the taxi, a woman ran toward us yelling, "Erika! Erika!" It was Don's mother, Flora, my new grandmother. It turns out that Don had to work later than he expected so he sent his mother to pick us up. Greatly relieved, we rode home to Sanford with Flora, her husband and her sister. Looking back now, the drive to Sanford must have been quite comical. The three of us were in the back-seat—Donna was still crying, I was throwing up, and Mom was carrying on in German trying to maintain some control over her children. I bet Grandma Flora was wondering what in the world her son had gotten himself into!

It did not take long for Mom to learn that Grandma Flora was the matriarch of the Whitten family, and she was very religious, as Don had previously explained to her. When Mom was pregnant with Donna, she received a letter from Flora introducing herself and in the letter she said that "in her country people got married *before* they had babies." In truth, Mom and Don probably would have already been married were it not for the problem with her birth certificate.

When we arrived at Grandma Flora's house, Don was waiting on the porch steps. He was thrilled to see us after almost a year of being apart. Mom wanted to run into his arms, but she didn't know how she should greet Don with Grandma Flora standing nearby, so she exercised great restraint. She walked up to him and politely stuck out her hand for him to shake.

Mother spent that night getting Donna and me bathed and tucked into bed. I can still remember my first bath in America in Grandma Flora's claw-foot bathtub. Everything was new — the food, the smells, American television, and the people, but we were too tired to care. Our first night ended well and most importantly, Mom and Don and Donna and I were finally together as a family.

We stayed at Grandma Flora's for just one night. Don had arranged for an apartment for us. All of Grandma Flora's friends, however, including most of the family, thought that Don and Erika were already married. Flora, being a fine and upstanding Christian woman, was not about to let her son live in sin, so first thing Monday morning she escorted my mother to the doctor's office to get a blood test. A few days later, with marriage license in hand, the three of them — Mom, Don, and Flora — drove to a little church in the nearby town of Longwood, where a private wedding ceremony quietly and promptly took place.

A short time later, Grandma Flora announced that the ladies from her church wanted to give Mom a belated bridal shower. Now Mom didn't know what a bridal shower was so she got out her English/German dictionary. She looked up the word "bridal." Mom understood that easy enough. Then she looked up the word "shower" and was a little surprised that these ladies, being so religious, would want to give her a bath and she wasn't sure what a bath had to do with being a bride. Grandma Flora had done her best to explain that she would receive all kinds of gifts for her new house, so Mom decided that she could tolerate anything for a short time. She remarked to Don, "Your customs are strange, but if those church ladies want to give me a shower, I'll go along with it for the gifts!" Don chuckled with delight at his new bride.

The *Leave It to Beaver* Years

It takes a special kind of man to love and raise another man's child. Don was that special kind of man. Within a few months after Don and my mom were married, he adopted me as his own. Not only did he give me his love, he also gave me a new last name, Andrea Dagmar Whitten. I grew up always knowing that I was adopted, especially since Grandma Flora used to introduce me proudly to her church friends as "Donny's little adopted daughter from Germany."

That made me feel special when she said that, but sometimes I realized that it made me different somehow. Even so, Don—who I will refer to as my dad—always accepted me, loved me, and made me feel like I was a part of him. Dad always introduced me as *his* daughter. He didn't see me any other way but as his own.

Our biggest hurdle in America was that neither Mom nor I spoke a word of English. Mom began to watch soap operas during the day while she did housework and that is how she learned English. Every day she would put us down for a nap and then tune in to *All My Children*. It seems funny now to think that Erica Kane taught Erika Whitten how to speak English. I, on the other hand, learned quickly from the children in our neighborhood and from going to school. I remember coming home sometimes and teaching Mother new words I had learned that day. Before long, we were both speaking English fluently.

Life was great in those early years. Dad had a good job with a successful company. He made a decent wage, enough to buy us a house with a big yard. Our house was small—800 square feet—but it was immaculate. Mother enjoyed taking care of our home. She was also good at stretching a dollar. Her lady friends would marvel at the things she could make without having to spend a lot of money for it. She had a flare for decorating—throw pillows, lacey drapes tied back with ribbons, fresh flowers in glass jars. She had a beautiful European style that neighbors would often compliment. Our home was comfortable and bright with Mother's special style.

We lived in a subdivision filled with lots of children and each day Donna and I were scooted out the front door to play. "Now go out and play and take your sister with you!" were the words I heard every morning. I was seven and Donna was four. I didn't want my baby sister hanging around, so I would run as fast as I could down the street, making sharp turns in and out of the neighbors' yards to lose her. On a good day, she would get lost in my trail and go back home. Donna and I shared a bedroom with a bunk bed, two dressers and a bookshelf that proudly displayed the baby dolls that Oma sent us from Germany.

I remember our schedule, too. We could set the world clock by our daily routine. Mother carefully planned dinner and preparations began about 3:00 in the afternoon. The house was spotless and the table was set for dinner by 4:00. By 4:45 Mother applied fresh lipstick and rubbed the smudges and dirt off our faces. We had to be neat and clean so we could jump into Dad's arms and not get his crisp white shirt dirty. Donna and I would lean over the couch and watch out the window for Dad to come home. Moments before he would arrive, Mother would stir up our excitement by saying, "Daddy will be here in a minute!" And sure enough, at 5:04 p.m. he would pull in the driveway in his burnt-orange 1957 Chevrolet. We couldn't wait to see him.

It was the same every day, with Dad's office just minutes away from the house. He walked through the doors, tousled our hair, loosened his tie, and gave Mom a kiss. She handed him a cold glass of sweet iced tea and we sat down for dinner at 5:05 p.m. Mom and Dad did most of the talking while Donna and I ate quietly. If either of them spoke to us it was usually to correct our table manners. Being good little girls, neither of us left the table until our plates were clean and we were given permission. Each evening ended the same, Donna and I taking a bath together and seeing who could make the biggest shampoo ball on our heads. By 7:30 p.m. Dad sent us off to bed with a kiss and then we'd whisper nonsense until we fell asleep.

Mother's Grand Entrance

My mom was a beautiful woman and she took good care of herself. She had an unmistakable European flair about her. The way she wore her hair and make-up, and the way she dressed, accentuated her natural beauty. She was a faithful customer to a neighbor who sold Avon products. Her hair was always "teased" and styled. Her nails were nicely manicured and polished. Mom would sunbathe in the backyard as Donna and I played in the sprinklers on summer days. Being it was the early 70's, Mom always wore a dress and pointed high heels, even to the grocery store.

Once when I was in the fifth grade, my teacher assigned me to bring a snack for class. I would have been happy to bring a bag of Oreos or something, but Mom reassured me that she would deliver something delicious to my class, maybe an apple pie or some cupcakes. I was so excited that she was making a visit to my school I didn't care what she brought. I could hardly concentrate that morning and found myself looking at the clock every few minutes. I couldn't wait for her to come to my classroom so I could see the reaction of my classmates.

Around 10:30 a.m., there was a knock on the door. My heart started to race, as I thought she was on the other side. The teacher opened the door and there she was. My mother made her grand entrance. She walked in carrying a tray covered in foil. She wore a light blue A-line dress to her knees. Around her small waist was a wide satin ribbon tied in a perfect bow. Her legs shimmered with a golden tan. Her high heels tapped on the floor as she walked across the room. In her German-Lithuanian accent, she said "Hello, I brought apple muffins for the class."

All the kids stared at her, intrigued by her accent and awed by her beauty. I could hear them whisper, "Wow, she's beautiful! Who is she?" I just sat there wiggling in my seat, not saying a word. Mom finished talking with the teacher and handed her the tray of muffins. As she turned to leave, she looked around the class and when she found me, Mom gave me a wink and waved good-bye. The class turned to me, asking, "Is that *your* Mom?" I was the proudest fifth-grader on the planet that day. "Yep, she's my mother!"

It sounds silly to make such a big deal about my mother coming to school. But some things just stick in your memory and that's one of those special moments I can't forget. There were many happy times in my early life. And many beautiful scenes like that of my mother. Those years were wonderful, maybe even close to perfect. The one thing that made it less than perfect was the fact that affection did not come easily for Mom. She seldom gave kisses and hugs.

I knew Mom loved me, because she showed it in many other ways, but I remember seeing how other mothers and daughters interacted with each other. I noticed they would greet each other with hugs and smiles and sometimes they even held hands. Other little girls got a goodnight kiss. That didn't happen with my mom. Looking back today as an adult, I can understand how she couldn't give something she never received herself. The impact of Mom's own childhood and lack of affection from Oma had been unknowingly passed on to her.

Still, those were the good times. I just didn't know how good they were until the winter of my sixth grade year, when my life took a nosedive. The bottom fell out of my parent's world and I watched everything good crumble before my eyes. What happened next was the beginning of the darkest days of my life.

Chapter Three

The Thief Comes

J ust before the holidays during the sixth grade, Dad came
home from work and announced that his company was
relocating to San Diego. They had given him the option of
moving us to California to keep his job or he could take
severance pay and look for new employment in our area.
Dad decided to take the severance pay and stay in Sanford.
He wanted to raise his family in his hometown and besides,
Donna and I were settled in school. But before we knew it,
Christmas was upon us and Dad had not had any luck finding
a new job.

A longtime friend of Dad's, Steve, owned a roofing business and offered Dad a temporary job on a roofing crew to
earn a few dollars just to get us through the holidays. Dad
accepted Steve's offer thinking he would do that for a little
while and then get back to looking for an office job. In only
a few short weeks, though, the hot Florida sun began to take
a toll on him.

Dad's body wasn't accustomed to the excessive heat
or the strenuous physical work. In no time at all, the sun
seemed to age him ten years. After long days on a 120-
degree rooftop, he came home in his tar-covered jeans and
work boots with no desire to sit down for dinner. He was

exhausted and wanted only to sit and cool off with an ice-cold beer. It usually took a few hours for him to build up an appetite for dinner.

A new pattern began to emerge in our lives as Dad started coming home after those long, hard days with a six-pack of beer. In the beginning, it was one beer to cool off and relax. Then one beer led to five more and eventually led to a second trip to the store for another six-pack. Before I knew it, Mom was having a beer with him. It didn't take long before the days ended with Mom and Dad both passed out cold on the couch. I watched his temporary job as a roofer turn from weeks into months, and then a year later, things got worse.

It was the following Christmas when the accident happened. By that time my parents were not only drinking every night, but during the day as well. Dad was driving one day after he had been drinking and he crashed into a semi-truck parked on the side of the road. Thankfully he wasn't seriously injured, but he totaled our car and knocked out his front teeth. Dad's driver's license was suspended for three years, which left our family with no transportation. Dad's dream of returning to an office job vanished and he never discussed it again.

The days of the crisp white shirts and dinner at 5:05 p.m. were a thing of the past. It was frustrating now to see my father as a manual laborer with a drinking problem, no car and no teeth. How could everything change so drastically in the span of one year? As I watched my parents' world collapse I felt helpless and angry with them for giving up so easily. Being only 12 years old, I wasn't capable of understanding all the dynamics of an adult world, but from my perspective it all seemed senseless. I was frustrated and convinced that it did not have to be this way.

The following year, my family's nightmare reached its pinnacle. It was hunting season and our family had gone on a hunting trip with my parent's friends. That night all the men sat around the bonfire talking about their big day in the woods and drinking beer. Dad evidently passed out and as he lay stretched out before the fire, one of his feet burned in his leather boot. He woke up to a numb foot and was unable to remove his shoe. His friends rushed him to the hospital to find his foot had melted in his boot. Dad had third-degree burns that required several skin grafts in order to save his foot. He was in the hospital for two months. That was two months of surgeries for him and it was two months with no income for our family.

When Dad got home from the hospital, our lives picked up right where they left off. Both of my parents were full-blown alcoholics by this time, and we were the "poor family" in the neighborhood. I could see the neighbors whispering and pointing as my mom or dad would walk to the 7-Eleven three blocks away and return with a six-pack and carton of cigarettes. The convenience store, where everything was drastically overpriced, became our new grocery store. I was ashamed of what our family had become and frustrated because I wanted so much more for them—and for me. I felt completely helpless, as their drinking affected everything in our lives.

Our house was neglected and falling apart by that time; the wood trim was rotting and the carport housed a junk car with flat tires. The lawn always needed cutting and weeds had grown into bushes. I remember one time out of shame and desperation, I used a pair of scissors to cut the grass near the front door. We didn't have air-conditioning so it was always hot and muggy in our house. I took showers to cool off and then Mom would yell at me for using too much water. There were never any clean towels and what towels there were, smelled of mildew because clean laundry sat in the basket for days waiting to be hung on the line.

Everything in our house reeked of cigarette smoke. Beer cans and cigarette ashes littered the kitchen counter and tables. Mom rarely cooked meals and when she did, it was some pot roast or stew that would go from the stove to the refrigerator for days. When the pot got low, she threw in a few more potatoes and carrots. I was so sick of eating that for breakfast. Milk was nonexistent in our house. How I longed to have a normal breakfast like other kids—a bowl of Fruit Loops with whole milk. Instead, on the rare occasions that Mom did shop, we got puffed rice with powdered milk.

The days of high school were the worst. I'd come home in the afternoons and find my mom sitting on the couch drinking and watching television, wasting the day away. In my frustration I'd say, "Mom, what are you doing?" She would just look at me with disgust and say, "Shut the hell up!" My beautiful mother, of whom I was once so proud, had turned into a cranky, mean drunk. It was as if our roles had reversed and I had become the adult fussing at her to get up and act like a mother should. I never came home to a happy greeting nor did Mom ever show any interest in my day. Our conversations consisted mainly of yelling at each other.

To be honest, some of it was probably my own fault because I was so disgusted with her and I lacked compassion and understanding. It would be years to come before I would learn about Jesus and the fact that I could let Him carry this burden for me. But until then, my youth and ignorance fought to make things right in my own strength. I didn't understand what alcoholism and depression looked like. All I understood was that my mother was being lazy and feeling sorry for herself. I just wanted her to get up and do the right thing—or just get up and do *something*. Instead, she sat and drank her life away.

In her drunken state, Mom would insult me and accuse me of trying to be someone I wasn't. She hated the way I looked, the way I dressed, the way I talked. She hated me being in her presence. I knew she despised me not only by the things she said to me, but by the way she looked at me.

On occasion, she would blurt out hateful comments about her life in Germany. Deep down, a part of me sensed that I was a living reminder of her past, of Germany, Oma—and even Giulio. There were a few occasions when I asked Mom about my real father, Giulio. Who was he? What did he look like?

In a hateful tone, she'd answer, "He's an SOB and looks like you, Andrea." So, when I'd look at myself in the mirror I wasn't sure if I should like what I saw. What was I supposed to think? Was I a bad person, too? Was I ever going to be good enough for my mother? I felt deep down I had so much to prove. She made it very clear how she felt about Giulio and I soon learned there was never a good time to bring up the subject. To keep the peace I eventually stopped asking anything about my biological father.

Because of her unresolved past, I felt she was taking it all out on me. It seemed I was on the receiving end of her drunken rage and anger. It was different with my little sister. Donna was three years younger than me and Mom didn't treat her the same way. She was affectionate toward her and even had a nickname for her, "Half-Pint." But then again, Donna wasn't fueling Mom's anger by asking questions about a man that she wanted to forget existed. I don't think Donna even realized the favor she had with Mom. If she did, she never flaunted it. The fact is Donna's life wasn't much easier than mine, so I never had any resentment toward my sister. And it wasn't like she was sticking out her tongue at me saying, "nah nah, boo boo…Mom loves me more."

No Signs of Life

Out of shame, I tried to hide the reality of my home life as much as I could. I never invited friends over. My parents' state of mind was too unpredictable and the last thing I wanted was for people to know what was really going on in our house. It was obvious to our neighbors and close relatives what was happening, but my friends at school got a different spin. Truthfully, I was afraid if they knew about my parents, they would reject me. I fought desperately to give the appearance we were living the *Leave It to Beaver* lifestyle. The facade wasn't difficult to maintain as long as no one ever came over.

Whereas I wanted to cover the shame of our home life, seeing Mom and Dad drunk did not seem to bother Donna as much. Because she was younger than me, I wondered if she remembered that we once had a better life. In some ways I tried to protect Donna from the reality of creditors calling us and from the lack of food by bringing home extra for her once I was working. When it was time to fill out the application for free school lunches, I forged our parent's signatures and instructed Donna to give the form to her teacher. For the most part, Donna and I were like any other sisters, getting into each other's belongings, fighting over dumb things one minute and then sticking together through a difficulty the next.

We both kept our home life private and did little to uncover what was really going on to teachers, neighbors or relatives. For example, if we saw Grandma Flora pull into the driveway for a visit, Donna and I would make a mad dash to grab all the empty beer cans and straighten up the living room before she reached the front door. Thankfully, we weren't victims of any sort of physical or sexual abuse. For the most part, Mom and Dad were quiet, functioning drunks content to go to work and then drink all night with little desire to rise above it.

During the ninth grade, there was a boy who was interested in me and wanted to call me, but I was too ashamed to tell him that our phone was disconnected. In order to save face, I gave him the phone number of the payphone at the 7-Eleven and told him to call me at a specific time. When the appointed time was near, I ran three blocks down the street and waited at the payphone for his call.

As with the phone service, we didn't always have full utility service. On occasion the water would get cut off, sometimes the electricity. When Dad got his paycheck on Fridays, he would go pay the bill, including late and reconnection fees, to get the power turned back on. There was a time when I was in high school that a date dropped me off at home around 8:00 in the evening. It was late enough to be dark, but too early for my parents to be in bed. When we pulled into the driveway, he asked why there weren't any lights on in the house. There were no lights because the power was shut off.

I said casually, "Oh, my parents are probably at a meeting and forgot to leave a light on." He then said, "Okay...I will wait here until you get in." That was a real mess trying to get him to leave, as there were no porch lights to turn on. After that, I never had anyone drive me to my house. They would drop me off at a nearby friend's house (I would make an excuse that I needed to pick up something) and then I'd walk the short distance home.

Of even deeper concern was the constant threat of mortgage creditors. However, just in the nick of time, like manna falling from heaven, Dad would have enough to make the house payment. We could breathe easy, at least until the next month and those precious "grace days" that bought us more time. I often thought, "Why does life have to be so hard?" I didn't hear my friends fretting about things like that.

I wished so often that someone would take me away from all of that chaos. I wanted to be cared for by responsible adults, instead of being the one to remind them the house payment was due, we needed bread, or the house needed cleaning. It was so frustrating to see the two people I loved just waste away. They didn't care about anything and stopped thinking like rational people. As I look back, I see that neither of them had good coping skills and when life handed them trials and tribulations, they chose to escape. They simply took another drink and gave up. I wish someone would have told the younger version of me this dark season of my life would eventually pass and that God had His eyes on me in the midst of it all.

The Summer of Big Bucks

As I entered my teen years, I realized that I needed to take responsibility for myself. I bought my own food, got myself to school and participated in many extracurricular activities. I got odd jobs to pay for my clothes. The summer before ninth grade was a great summer. Steve, Dad's boss, and his wife, Ann, asked me to baby-sit their three children for the summer. Steve, Ann and my dad grew up together in the same town and attended the same high school. They were good friends of our family and were more aware than I thought of our chaotic home life and generously opened their home to give me a break.

They were a wonderful family and I loved them dearly. Steve and Ann did what they could to help my parents see what they were doing with their lives. Unfortunately, Mom and Dad were not convinced they had a problem. That particular summer, I would go over to Steve and Ann's house on Sunday night and stay with them until Friday night. I was thrilled with that arrangement because the less I was home, the better. I'm sure my mother was relieved too, not having me around to nag her.

Steve and Ann left early in the mornings for work and I ran their house smoothly and efficiently during the day. I had the kids out of bed, dressed, fed, teeth brushed, hair combed, beds made, dishes washed, laundry done and carpets vacuumed, with plenty of time left to chat on the phone with my friends. The best part was on Friday afternoon when Ann handed me $45. Forty-five big ones! I couldn't believe that every week they paid me that kind of money. It was BIG money for a 15-year-old in the mid-70s.

The truth was I would have done it for free just to get to spend those three months with them and to live in their world. When they came home from work, Ann would prepare dinner and then everyone sat around the table like a family to eat together. Steve and Ann loved hearing about our day. After everyone had a bath, we'd sit in the living room and watch sitcoms like *Happy Days* and *Laverne and Shirley* until 11:00 p.m. Then Steve would get up and say, "Okay kids, fun's over. It's time to hit the hay!" We'd all go to bed and I couldn't wait to get up the next day and do it all over again.

Occasionally, I would overhear Ann talking on the phone with her sisters and she would be bragging about me. She'd tell them how much she appreciated me and all that I did for her and her family. I felt special and valued doing something important and needed. Ann wasn't happy about going to work and being away from her children, but she had great confidence in me and often expressed her appreciation. Sometimes in the evenings, she would invite me to run errands with her. She was like the mother I wished I had. She was sober and liked to talk to me. It felt good knowing someone cared about how I felt or what I had to say.

After that summer was over, I had a stack of cash that could choke a horse. I spent three weekends at Zayres, the '70s equivalent of Wal-Mart or Target. I bought a full wardrobe for school. I had ten pairs of shoes and jeans in every color. I bought sweaters and blouses to mix and match, purses, makeup and perfume. I even had enough money left over to hook up my own telephone in my bedroom. When Mom or Dad needed to make a call, they would come in my room and ask if they could borrow my phone. I would chuckle and say, "Just leave a quarter by the bed!" I got a kick out of knowing they needed *my* phone.

When school started, I felt like a Rockefeller with all the new clothes I had. I could go for three weeks without wearing the same outfit. I felt so proud and good about myself because, in some ways, my new wardrobe made up for the body I didn't have. I was a skinny girl, I mean *really* skinny. But it wasn't because I didn't eat. I just had a very high metabolism. I was very self-conscious of my body, as most girls are, but my body looked lanky and lacked any developing curves. I didn't even develop breasts until I was in the ninth grade.

I was always the brunt of the "flat-chested" jokes at school. They'd call me from behind, "Hey, Andrea, turn around so we can see your back," or "You're a pirate's dream—a sunken chest!" In eighth grade, I made a huge mistake and wore a padded bra to school. I wore it with a tight lime-green sweater to show off the curves. I made a real idiot of myself. Two girls noticed the "overnight miracle" and laughed nonstop for days every time they saw me in the halls. I should have known better—you don't just show up at school one day with new breasts! To say the least, I was a late bloomer. That's why a closet full of new clothes was a small consolation for the "late blossoming" to a certain extent.

A Real Job

Once I was in tenth grade I got a job at a family-owned chicken restaurant that kept their "famous recipe" chicken a real mystery. The owner never even told the employees about this highly protected patent for fear we'd spill the beans. The owner was a very *thrifty* man. He paid us minimum wage, worked us like slaves and would even make us pay for our meals on dinner breaks. I shamefully admit that when our miserly boss would make his daily run to the bank, we would eat his chicken and lick up his honey packs as fast as we could. When break time came, we'd just sit in a booth and drink some water.

The next step up the corporate ladder was McDonald's. I worked there for about three months before my next move, which was a cashier at Fairway Markets. There were only three grocery stores in Sanford and Fairway Markets was the one I had my sights set on. I loved being a cashier there. I worked at Fairway Markets through high school and my first year in college. Soon after I started, I got to work in the coveted office position with the assistant manager. I cashed checks for customers, processed money orders and balanced the cash drawers every night. It was great until the day there was a $500 shortage in the vault and everyone who worked in the office had to take a polygraph test.

I was scared to death to take the polygraph. I didn't steal the $500, but I had stolen a boatload of other stuff from the store. I knew my crimes would make that polygraph needle wiggle off the chart. When all the testing was over, they discovered who took the $500, so I was off the hook for that, but my manager, Mr. Brooks, called me into his office to talk to me about the other stolen items I revealed in my confession.

"Yes, Mr. Brooks, I've stolen shampoo, deodorant, breakfast bars, cans of ravioli, and countless candy bars and beef jerky. What was I supposed to do? I couldn't afford them." I had been too embarrassed to ask for help or to tell anyone I needed basic hygiene goods and food. I cried and begged Mr. Brooks to give me another chance. I shamefully told him about my home life, that there wasn't always food and other necessities in my house, and what money I did make, I needed to pay my car payment and insurance.

I pleaded, "I'm sorry, Mr. Brooks. I'm not trying to make excuses for what I did. I now understand just how serious this is and there is no excuse for stealing." I wept as I realized the trust that was broken. How would they ever trust me in the office if I was stealing store merchandise? I never intended to tell anyone about my home life, especially an employer. But I am glad that I did because I found that the saying is true—confession *is* good for the soul. Regardless of the consequences I was to face, sharing my story with Mr. Brooks was cathartic. I released years of pent-up emotions and frustration and I was amazed to discover what a relief it was to get some of that poison out of me.

What happened next was nothing short of a miracle. Mr. Brooks gave me another chance. He said he would give me more hours if I promised not to steal anymore. I made that promise and I kept it. Knowing about my family life changed everything. If another employee called in sick, Mr. Brooks always called me first to see if I could work. He even asked me to baby-sit his kids several times when I wasn't at the store. That really meant a lot to me, and it means even more to me today as a parent. Looking back, I am extremely thankful for the incredible grace Mr. Brooks showed me, especially when I didn't deserve it. Like Steve and Ann, Mr. Brooks was one of those people that stood in the gap for me. He showed me I didn't have to settle for the way things were. He gave me a second chance and encouraged me to excel in life.

Freedom

As my parents were stuck in a world of despair and hopelessness, I avoided coming home. I seldom saw Donna, who had started hanging out with some bad kids in the neighborhood. In some ways, I felt like I had failed as a big sister in protecting her from the direction she was heading.

I filled my days with classes, clubs, and friends, while my nights were busy with work and football games. I enjoyed every minute of my high school life. Besides the school clubs, I was on the dance team, the drama team, and the yearbook and newspaper staffs. I was even a sports trainer. I loved my life—my life away from home, that is. My home life and my school life were two separate worlds. And once I had my own car—a 1970 Ford Maverick (with duct-taped floorboards) that cost me $350—I had a new sense of freedom. I wasn't dependent on anyone else for rides, but could come and go as I pleased.

As I look back at my high school days, I can see that God was looking out for me; for once again He brought a special person into my life to motivate and encourage me. Mrs. Epps was my drama teacher and in my senior year, I became her assistant, grading papers and running errands for her. At least a couple times a week, we went off campus to Pizza Hut for lunch. A friend of mine and another teacher would come along also. As my friendship with Mrs. Epps grew over the years, she even hired me to baby-sit her four-year-old daughter on production nights.

First "Real" Boyfriend

I met another special person in my sophomore year. A friend invited me to a party that her older brother was having. Her brother and his friends had all graduated from the same high school we were attending. Paul, one of her brother's friends, was the quiet one in the bunch. Paul had a warm smile and a quiet confidence about himself. He was 18 years old and attended a local community college. I felt really immature around Paul and thought for certain I would never have a chance with him. If anything, I felt as though I annoyed him with my silly antics and over-bubbly personality. I did most of the talking that night, but by the end of the evening—to my surprise—he asked for my phone number.

The next day, Paul called me. He picked me up in his car and we went to the high school and talked for two hours sitting on the football stadium bleachers. He was the nicest guy I had ever met—interesting and witty and seemed to know what he wanted in life. I was very comfortable with Paul and enjoyed talking with him. Paul officially became my "first love." He knew everything about me and my life, and amazingly, nothing about my home life scared him off.

Paul lived with his widowed uncle and they had a very good relationship. They were like two bachelors living together. When I was around, they both treated me like a queen. His uncle was very kind and I could see where Paul's good character came from. He didn't hang out with friends his own age very often, as most of them gave him a hard time for dating a high school girl. But Paul was his own man and didn't need anyone's approval. I liked that about him. He didn't care what his friends thought of me. And the more I was with Paul, the less I felt the dark cloud of alcoholic parents hanging over my head.

Paul and I dated all through my high school years. He accompanied me to two homecoming dances and my junior and senior prom. He came to all the games and watched me perform on the dance team and was always there for me. The nights I wasn't working at Fairway Markets, I was usually at his house. We'd watch television, do our homework and have dinner with his uncle. I became like the lady of the house. He was very good to me, very protective and gentle. Paul loved me and as our relationship deepened and our affection became more intimate, he respected my fear of becoming sexually active and did not pressure me.

Pomp and Circumstance

My parents only came to two of my high school events. One was my graduation and the other was the Miss Seminole pageant. During my senior year, the Anchor Club nominated me to be Miss Seminole High School. The first night of the pageant was a talent contest and I did a monologue. The second night was the evening gown and interview portion of the contest. A panel of teachers judged our speaking ability and questioned our academic goals. For the interview, our instructions were to come center-stage one at a time, stand behind the microphone and thoughtfully answer the questions given. We were to look dignified and told, "After the last question, stand still and silently count to thirty before you leave the stage." I was especially nervous because I was the first contestant.

After answering the last question, I stood still and began to count silently. The lights were so bright that I couldn't see beyond the judges' chairs. There was an awkward silence in the audience and it felt like the seconds lingered for hours. The audience seemed uncomfortable also and wondered why I was just standing there. Feeling like an idiot and counting in my head, I heard a lone pair of hands clapping. I adjusted my eyes to see beyond where the judges sat. I found my dad standing in the audience and saw that he was the source of the singular applause. It seemed as if he had felt my discomfort and awkwardness and wanted to make me feel better, so he broke the silence for me. I wasn't crowned Miss Seminole, but I felt as special as if I'd won because of Dad being there.

Another sweet memory of Dad happened around the time of senior prom. Prom was one of the biggest events of my senior year and, of course, the biggest part of prom for any girl is getting a dress. A few months before the dance, I found the perfect dress. It cost $110. That was a lot of money, but I really liked it, so I asked Dad if he could help me buy it.

I knew he didn't have much money and he made no promises that he would be able to, so I didn't get my hopes up. In the event that Dad couldn't come through I had a backup plan—a used dress from a friend. The week before prom Dad surprised me with the entire amount and asked me not to tell Mom about it. I never figured out how he pulled it off when he only made $200 a week, but I was truly grateful for the sacrifice he made for me.

By my senior year, Paul finished his second year of college and went into the Air Force so he was gone most of the time. Before he left, he asked me to marry him. Our plans were to marry after I graduated and move to where he would be stationed. In the beginning I missed him greatly and we wrote letters often and talked about the days following my graduation. I kept busy in my senior year with all my extracurricular activities and my job. I didn't have plans for college as I didn't have the money or the academic grades to get a scholarship. It seemed there was really no need to consider college anyway, since I was going to marry Paul and he would take me away to a better life.

However, my plans for the future took a turn when I was encouraged by Mrs. Epps to apply for a scholarship offered by the local Women's Pilots Club. They were looking for a promising student that needed a financial break. I applied for the scholarship with a glowing recommendation from Mrs. Epps. Three months before graduation the Pilot's Club awarded me a two-year scholarship. I never imagined I was good enough to go to college and recall racing to Fairway Markets to tell my boss, Mr. Brooks. He was so proud of me.

The thought of going to college changed everything. I began to question if I was really ready to marry Paul—even if I waited until after college. During his absence, I realized that I didn't miss him as much as I thought. I felt awful and even guilty for feeling that way. I shared my feelings with Mrs. Epps one day and she challenged me to search my heart to see if I loved Paul the same way he loved me. I soon realized that I didn't love him in a romantic way, but more like a big brother or a special friend. I think Paul was more of a rescuer to me than a future husband. I felt safe and comfortable with him and our relationship was easy and required very little of me. In some ways, I was too dependent on him. And though he was good to me, he wasn't good *for* me. What I really needed was to be out on my own to "spread my wings" and learn to stand on my own.

It was a painful and tearful breakup over the phone. Paul normally called me on Sunday evenings from the base. That particular Sunday, I dreaded taking his call. After hours of talking, he pleaded with me to reconsider and take more time before making a final decision. I knew in my heart that I needed to let Paul go. He was such a good man and deserved more than what I was capable of giving him. While I was sick to my stomach with the thought of not having the security of Paul in my life, I also knew I would be holding on to him for the wrong reasons.

A couple of months after I graduated Paul came home on leave and we said our goodbyes in person. Paul was an incredible young man, so kind and understanding. He reassured me that we were doing the right thing and that he never regretted the time we had together. As I look back, I can see how God put Paul in my life specifically for that season of time.

Chapter Four

Finding My Way

There was a genuine sense of freedom after graduating high school and ending my long relationship with Paul. Even though I was still living at home and working at Fairway Markets, the difference now was that I had a future—a future with me standing on my own. Attending college was an idea that I had never imagined. In our family, the subject of higher education didn't exist. If anything, they criticized me for trying to better myself or as they put it, "pretending to be someone you're not."

By this time, Donna was 16 years old and had met Gilbert. He was 19 years old and had recently moved into our neighborhood with his family. Gilbert came from a good Christian family and was the best thing that ever happened to Donna. He and his family introduced Donna to church and it wasn't long before Donna committed her life to Jesus and later fell in love with Gilbert.

After a year of dating, they got married—with Mom and Dad's permission, since she was a minor. At first I thought she was getting married to get out of the house and to quit school, but Gilbert saw to it that she finished high school. (I am happy to tell you today that Donna and Gilbert have been married 25 years and have two wonderful children, Cameron and Amber.)

The summer before I began college, I worked as many hours as I could at the market to save money for my own place. I dated a few guys off and on, but nothing serious. I enjoyed my freedom and wasn't eager to get serious with anyone. I felt good about myself and liked the attention I got from other guys, but I was very selective about whom I dated. One thing I noticed after graduating high school was that people seemed to judge me less on my parent's merits once they saw me making my own plans. What my parents were doing with their lives started to have less of an impact on me for the most part, with one exception.

Dennis was the son of a prominent businessman in our town. We had known each other throughout high school. His father was in the construction industry and was very successful. Dennis and I had dated for a couple of weeks when he invited me to a barbeque at his family's beach condo.

We spent a beautiful summer day on the beach and boating. That evening, Dennis and I joined his family for a patio dinner. As I filled my plate with chicken and baked beans, his mother and I had a friendly exchange. She asked about my interests and my future plans for college. Everything was going well until the subject turned to my family pedigree. I tried my best to dodge the questions about my family, especially when she asked me, "What does your father do?" I looked around for Dennis to return with his plate and rescue me from his mother's interrogation.

"He's in the construction business," I said quickly. On the inside, I could see where this was heading. The stage was being set for judgment.

"Oh…what kind of business?" she asked in a polite yet relentless tone.

"The roofing business," I replied, knowing exactly what she was getting at.

"Oh...does he own his own roofing company?"

"No," I paused and then added, "Actually, he's a roofer."

"Ohhhh..."

By my second year of college, I lived on my own sharing a two-bedroom apartment with three roommates. College life wasn't bad, except that I didn't get much sleep and it seemed I never had any money. Having three roommates limited any time for privacy, sleep, food or clean clothes. It was like having three little sisters who were sucking the life out of me and my wallet as it seemed I was the only one who ever bought shampoo or laundry detergent.

Although I loved the freedom, the novelty of living on my own began to wear thin. I enjoyed not knowing what my parents were doing, but the freedom came with a price. Working, studying, and living on Ramen noodles wasn't all it was cracked up to be. I asked Mr. Brooks for more hours at the market. He was very good to me and did his best to work around my college classes. But I needed more money and it wasn't beneath me to get my hands dirty, so I started cleaning two houses a week. Between the two jobs, I still had barely enough to cover my rent, car payment, insurance, gas, and food.

To my dismay, my financial situation required me to crawl back to my parent's world temporarily. I felt like a puppy with its tail between its legs. They didn't mind me coming back; I just had to endure the "I told you so" digs. At home, not much had changed, except for me. Mom and Dad were drinking more. They still didn't have a car or any plans to improve their lives. Dad was still working on the roof and Mom had found a job at a plant nursery. They came home in the evenings exhausted and found relief in a case of beer. By

9:00 p.m. they were passed out and then up the next morning for another round of the same thing.

Between my college classes and job at the market, I was seldom home except for showers and sleep. The upside of being home was that rent was free, so I had a few months to save money for my next move, which would be for good. Now that I had experienced independence and self-sufficiency, I was more determined not to come home again.

Invitation

One night during my second year of college, a friend of mine, Sue, invited me to a Bible study she had recently joined. Sue and I had been friends since grade school and she lived just a block from my parent's house. We graduated from high school together and now we were attending the same community college. I spent many summer days at Sue's house when we were younger.

She had the best Barbie doll collection—and the best record collection. We'd play her old vinyl records for hours and our teen idols came alive. Our favorites were Donny Osmond and Andy Gibb. We had it all planned out. She was going to marry Donny and I was going to marry Andy. She had life-size posters plastered on her walls and we'd lie on her twin beds and dream about our futures as Mrs. Osmond and Mrs. Gibb!

The new Bible study she invited me to was all Sue could talk about. She was crazy about this guy named David (not in a romantic way) who also attended the study. Sue thought David was funny and had a great sense of humor. He had recently become a Christian and was fired up about his new faith. The small home group was part of a Pentecostal organization that formed small study groups in homes.

They offered a class called "Power for Abundant Living" and they taught that after six weeks of this study, you *would* be filled with the Holy Spirit and *would* be speaking in tongues. "They'd be speaking *what*?" I asked Sue. I didn't understand it. She told me the class cost $25 and their goal was to get people to take the class and commit their lives to Jesus.

It seemed harmless enough so I accepted her offer and decided to attend the study with her. I figured I had nothing to lose and was not opposed to getting a little Jesus into my life. The Bible study was held in DeBary, a retirement community next to our town. Once I got there, it didn't take long to figure out whom David was. He immediately captured my attention—and my heart! The moment he welcomed me to the study I fell head over heels for him.

He was real, engaging, transparent and handsome. He was magnetic, passionate about life and his zeal for the Lord was contagious. I kept thinking, *Is this guy for real? Is there such a thing as love at first sight? Would I look like a complete idiot if I went up to him and said, "Will you marry me, father my children and grow old with me?"* I never did, but the thought crossed my mind.

After the Bible study ended that night, David and some of the others in the group asked me if I wanted to go to a local pub for sodas and to play pool. I thought that seemed strange—Christians going into a pub for a soda. That I had to see. The stereotype I held of Christians was that of straight-laced folks afraid to laugh out loud, never mind going into a pub. As everyone else shot pool that night, David and I sat at a table and talked. He told me about his conversion, his family and some of his interests. His enthusiasm was exhilarating and I, too, became very interested in what he had to say.

He shared God's truths and the hope he had in Jesus with me. I soon learned about God's unconditional love and that my inadequacies didn't matter to Him. I recall thinking, *God loves me like I am?* All these years I had tried to prove myself, hoping others would not look down on me because I was the daughter of alcoholics. To hear that God loved me *for me* was refreshing. Some of what he said about what Jesus did for me on the cross was beginning to come back to me. As a young girl, I had attended Grandma Flora's church enough to know the basics principles of Christianity. But back then I found the idea of being a Christian unappealing.

It seemed that all I ever heard about was what a person *can't* do or *shouldn't* do as a Christian—no dancing, no movies, no bathing suits, and no going to the pubs. I thought Christians were boring and more like zombies with no thought of their own. All I ever heard was the legalism behind Christianity, and little of grace and mercy. I never heard anything in church presented from an angle of freedom, freedom to be the person and personality that God created me to be or that God delighted in the individual person that He had created in each of us. David had an incredible way of seeing Christianity as real and personal. His explanation of a personal relationship with Jesus versus religion appealed to me.

After an engaging three-hour conversation with David, I wanted to hear more. To be honest, I was very interested in him, too. He was 26 and I was 20, but I knew that night he was the man I would someday marry. He was my soul mate. Now, whether he recognized that was yet to be determined.

I learned that night that David and his family were from Cleveland, Ohio. I asked him, "So what brought you to a retirement community in Florida at the age of 26?" David was born and raised in Ohio, the youngest of four. He had two older sisters and one brother. When David was four years old, a drunk driver killed one of his sisters at age 16. His parents were in their 60s (whereas my parents were only in their 40s). David had been an unexpected pregnancy for his mom at the age of 40. His oldest sister was the same age as my parents.

He explained that his mom and dad worked for a recording company in Ohio and had two years left before they could retire, but they decided to buy a house in Florida. They asked if David would move into their Florida house rent-free and occupy it for two years while they finished working. He accepted their offer and moved to Florida planning to return to Ohio when they retired. In less than a year of living in his parent's retirement home, David met his friends from the Bible study group.

For the next few weeks, I continued going with Sue to the Bible study. For the first time in my life, I read the Bible and began to pray daily. I made a confession of faith and accepted Jesus as my personal Savior. I could not wait until our weekly meetings. It was wonderful to share what we were learning as well as each other's burdens. But one thing I learned was that the group wasn't too excited about any budding romantic relationships. It was a tight-knit bunch and dating was not on their agenda. So, as my fondness for David grew, I played it cool and kept my feelings to myself. I didn't even tell Sue. Examining my heart, I often asked myself, "Was I here for discipleship or David?" The truth was both.

I was growing close to God and I came to the realization of God's love for me and that He had a plan for my life. A plan, by the way, that far exceeded what I could have ever imagined. God revealed to me that I did not have to settle for less or accept the lifestyle my parents were mired in. He has given each of us a free will and the ability to make our own choices. With my eyes on God, He would help me overcome everything, including my past.

As for David being a part of that plan, I knew that was a matter in which I would have to trust God. I asked God to protect my heart and help me hold on loosely to David as I could sense a tug of war beginning. The group leaders had big plans for David. They were grooming him (as well as Sue) to go to the mission field. Any heartstrings tugging at David would be a distraction to the calling. David had an evangelistic spirit and was excited about going. He loved sharing his faith and it came natural for him.

The purpose of sending missionaries was to spread the good news of the gospel, which, of course, wasn't a new concept. They were looking for people who would commit one year of their lives to serve as a missionary, or ambassador, to spread the gospel and plant a new home group in a new community. Each summer, the new ambassadors would meet at a national convention and be assigned their destination somewhere in the United States. Their assignment included partnering with three or four other ambassadors whom would all meet for the first time at the convention.

Everyone came to the convention with their bags packed, no more than $300 in cash, and ready to meet their new "family" and be commissioned into the mission field. They didn't know until then what would be their destination. It was a little scary, while at the same time exciting, and it required a leap of faith and complete trust in God to provide for all their needs. The home group I attended was the result of four people who made that same commitment one year earlier. At first, the whole arrangement sounded a little strange to me and I asked a lot of questions.

The assignment lasted from August 1 through July 31 of the following year. The new family would establish a residence in a house or an apartment with a one-year lease. Each member had to be at least 18 years old and could work no more than 30 hours a week at a regular job. They made it clear that the focus of the mission was to establish a home group and not a career move. The idea was to work just enough to be able to live and with everyone sharing the expenses, it was manageable.

Forbidden Love

Besides receiving solid discipleship at the Bible studies I attended, the group always did fun things together. If the group went on a picnic, I was invited. If the group went to the movies, I was invited. When the group went to the beach, I was invited. And usually David called me to make sure I was coming along. At all these outings, I was by David's side constantly. If we went out to eat, I sat next to him. When it was time to pray, I wanted to be the one next to him to hold his hand. I tried not to look so obvious, but I was crazy in love with David. I thought he liked me, but I knew he was not in a position to make any overtures. If anything, David seemed guarded with how he felt about me. We didn't talk about his plans after the mission, but he did say he wanted my assurance that I would keep in touch with him while he was gone.

Within months, it was no secret that David and I had developed a special bond, but it was not a relationship that could be defined. I saw the leaders of the group begin to tire of my presence at the meetings. They viewed me as a distraction to David and felt threatened that I would mess up the plans they had for their "golden boy," as he shared with me later that they'd had many private talks with him. They stressed the importance of us staying focused on God and not getting caught up in the "flesh." I had mixed feelings about their concerns. How could falling in love with David not be in God's plans?

Our attraction to each other was very controlled. When the group met, everyone always greeted each other with holy kisses and hugs, and David's hugs were especially snug—the kind in which I just wanted to lose myself. But because we never were alone, we were protected from each other's true admiration. Until one day out of the blue, when David called me and asked, "I was wondering if you'd like to go see a movie tonight?"

My response came quickly, "Sure! What does everyone want to see?"

"No, just you and me," he said. My heart skipped a beat. It was the day I had been waiting for. I would finally get to be alone with him and not have all those eagle eyes peering at my every move. Trying to collect my composure, I calmly responded.

"Just you and me? Are we allowed to do this? Will the group mind?"

"I'm a grown man. I don't need the group's approval to ask you out."

David's response couldn't have been more perfect. He was his own man. My heart was pounding. There was hope for us after all! Don't get me wrong, I didn't have any intention of getting between him and God's plan for his life. It was his love and passion for the Lord that had attracted me to him in the first place. I loved being around a man that loved the Lord and treated women with respect. I certainly didn't want to become a stumbling block for him. I just wanted to be a part of his life, too.

He said he'd pick me up at my house at 6:00 p.m. I couldn't wait to finally spend time with David alone. Then my mind flashed into the future and I quickly realized there was one huge problem. One potential hazard that could possibly mess everything up for me was my obnoxious, alcoholic parents. I was still living at my parent's house and David would have to meet them. They always made fun of the guys I dated. Would they scare off my beloved David or would it even matter to him? I had to remind myself that David was a grown man and that I came this far on my own merits. Early on, in one of our many conversations, I alluded to the fact that my parents were a little strange, so he was slightly forewarned.

From my vagueness and discomfort, he would have had every right to be cautious, if not intimidated. What was he going to think of them? Of me? I wondered, once again, if there would ever come a day when I would be seen for who I was and not judged as a product of my parents or the environment in which I lived. Would David take one look at them and reconsider dating a girl from *The Beverly Hillbillies*? Moments before his arrival, I was stricken with fear, but I accepted the fact that this could be the deal-breaker.

Well, the meeting went exactly as expected. "Granny" and "Uncle Jed" totally embarrassed me. Thank God David was such a good sport and laughed when my mother greeted him. The first thing she said to him was, "You smell like a French whore!" I quickly snapped back at her, "That's what someone clean smells like!" David just smiled and even seemed amused by it all. The pleasantries lasted about five painful minutes.

David shook my father's hand and said, "It's a pleasure to meet you. If it's okay, Andrea and I are going to see a movie now." David took my hand and we went out to his car. He opened the door for me and as he walked around to the driver's side he waved back at "Granny" who was standing at the door. When he got in the car, we looked at each other and laughed (and we've been laughing ever since). Today, he still jokes about it all the time. David tells people he was convinced I came from money—with all the beer cans lying around my parent's house, he was sure I must have been the heiress to a brewery fortune.

Our first date was the movie *On Golden Pond* with Henry Fonda and Katherine Hepburn. Our favorite line was when Katherine told Henry "he was her knight in shining armor." After the movie, we went to a café for coffee and talked for hours. David shared his heart with me and told me he had feelings for me. He made no promises, but assured me that he wanted me to wait for him to return from his mission trip.

We sealed our date with a kiss—and that one was no holy kiss! I floated on a cloud for days.

David and I continued to see each other on the nights that our group was not meeting and made it a point not to draw attention to ourselves while we were with them. I felt so comfortable sharing with David my hopes and dreams, the shame of my family background and even about the biological father I never knew. None of that seemed to matter to him. It was so nice to be free to talk about anything and even laugh at most of it with him. He often expressed his fascination and admiration of who I had become despite it all.

Two months after our first date, the church leaders commissioned the love of my life to Lynchburg, Virginia. Sue, who had also made the commitment to go to the mission field, was assigned to Dallas, Texas. I continued to attend the home study after they left. One of the group leaders stayed in our area to help develop a stronger group before he went back home. Our small group prayed often for David and Sue's mission assignments. It was comforting to have the group there, as I missed David terribly. College, working at the market part-time and cleaning three houses a week helped pass the time.

We wrote letters to each other daily. Going to the mailbox was the highlight of my day. David got a job in an electronics store. He shared with me his day-to-day challenges and what was happening with his new family members and even what drove him crazy about them. A blessing from God early on was one of the guys got a job at a local steakhouse. Every night he'd come home with a platter of steaks that were "overcooked" along with a bucket of rice pilaf. They ate like royalty. After a few weeks, though, the novelty of eating steak for every meal grew old.

David and his "family" started a small group in their home and invited new people. Things moved along pretty well in the early months, but by the fifth month, David was showing signs of distress. He tried to follow their instructions, but started to sense something bad. Some things that seemed a little peculiar about this organization made David nervous. He heard some criticism by Protestant denominations that the group was a cult. While David was excited about evangelizing and doing his part, the Bible study group seemed more interested in signing people up for their $25 class. When David took his concern to the leaders, they told him to either sign people up for the class or wipe the dust off his feet and go to the next person.

The money, it seemed, had become more important than the truths they taught. David began to question his calling and why he had been sent out. In his letters, I saw his discouragement and I knew his zeal was gone. Feeling like an outsider, he just wanted to come home. The others in his group chastised him and told him he was "wigging out." They used that term when someone was going AWOL. He had become a detriment to the group and it soon appeared the best thing would be for David to leave. So he packed his bags and drove home to Florida.

A Broken Heart

When David returned, he seemed like a different person. There was a spirit of sadness about him. He had been through quite an ordeal—enough to shake the foundations of his faith. He was more skeptical and cautious in his approach to life. He was quiet and needed time to reflect and make sense of it all. It was as if he had been through a brainwashing and needed time to recover. This whole experience had a deep spiritual impact on both of us.

Being a baby Christian myself, I had a difficult time understanding all of this. I started to question if God was real in my life. Was everything I learned a lie? As we spent time talking, David reassured me that God is real and He can be trusted. What we came to understand from it was that David and I were led astray by an organization that wanted to profit from God by manipulating naïve followers like ourselves.

Even with all the changes, I was very much in love with David and felt a heart connection like I had never experienced before. What I felt for David was powerful and grew deeper every day. We continued to pray and lean on God for strength and wisdom for our future. We didn't replace the organization with any kind of group or church, but tried to keep our focus on God while avoiding any outside influence since it hurt too much.

When I look back at those early days of my faith, I am grateful that God is in the business of healing hearts no matter the source of the wound. He took a bad experience and turned it into a life lesson for me. God brought me to a saving knowledge of Jesus through a wayward religious organization with selfish motives. He does whatever it takes for a soul to come to Him and He has the amazing ability to make all things new. Even though our faith was shaken, we learned the importance of worshiping God and not man.

Chapter Five

The Balancing Act

Within eight months of his returning home, David and I were married. We waited until Sue returned from her mission trip so she could be my maid of honor since she introduced us. Unlike David's experience on the mission field, hers was a positive one. Not only was having Sue at our wedding special, but we also had Oma (my grandmother from Germany) there, too. Although it had been 20 years since Mom and I left Germany, the two of them kept in touch with occasional letters each year, each of Mom's letters inviting Oma to come visit us in America. Five years earlier, Oma made her first trip to see us, and on her second visit, she stayed six weeks and was able to be at our wedding.

Our wedding was small and intimate. We were married in Grandma Flora's church, the one that I had visited often as a young girl. I have to admit while some brides may sing the popular song "Get Me to the Church on Time," my rendition that day was "Get My Parents to the Church Sober!" I was quite anxious about them showing up late and intoxicated.

On August 27, 1983, with me wearing a white, off-the-shoulder tea-length dress and a veil with a dainty crown of roses made for me by Grandma Flora, David and I said our "I dos" and I was the happiest woman in the world.

My parents arrived on time and they were both sober. Dad cleaned up nice in a tuxedo and walked me down the aisle. The ceremony was traditional and we had a garden reception at David's parents' house with an open bar that my parents bellied up to without a moment's hesitation. At that point, I really didn't care what happened. I was Mrs. David Krazeise and nothing else mattered.

David had done his homework and planned a beautiful honeymoon on the shores of St. Augustine at Amelia Island. It was like stepping out of ordinary life into a dream. Chilled champagne, rose petals, tennis, horseback riding, and long walks on the beach highlighted our week as we planned our lives and future together. We enjoyed our honeymoon so much we went back on our fifth wedding anniversary and did it all over again.

After returning from our honeymoon, we took our wedding gift money and shopped for new furniture. Those were fun days as we decorated our one-bedroom apartment and made it our home. I don't think I had my mother's flare for decorating but I knew how to take some milk crates and turn them into functional end tables. With some lounge furniture, added throw pillows, we lived like kings.

As we settled into married life, I finished college with a summer course and continued to clean houses. David worked full-time as a manager for an auto repair shop that specialized in European cars. For the first three years of our married life, we lived in an apartment with the dream of one day owning our own home. Our income was meager; however, we lived within our means and managed to save a little money each month. David and I realized early on that we did not have parents to financially lean on, so we were very frugal. Around this time, David's father died of cancer at age 70, leaving David's mom alone.

With a two-year college degree under my belt, I thought it was time to pursue a career with a future and something more satisfying than cleaning houses. My first career job took me to a bank as a teller. I had wanted to work in an office or business atmosphere so the bank seemed like a perfect setting for me. However, the job was a bust in less than six months. As a bank teller, accuracy was essential and my cash drawer never seemed to balance. One day it would be 20 cents over, the next day 82 cents short. I couldn't understand why I was having such a hard time balancing my drawer, while at Fairway Markets I had to balance my cash drawer every day and was on the mark every time.

Before getting the boot from that bank, I applied for a job at the bank next door. I was so thankful they did not call my previous bank for a reference. The new teller position was at a well-established savings and loan that had existed in our town for 35 years. Amazingly, I did great and managed to balance my cash drawer every day. Eager to make a good impression with upper management, my confidence grew as well as my professional image.

Within a year, I became a teller trainer and in addition to training all the new tellers, I worked on writing an extensive policy and procedure manual for the teller department. I had learned from our internal auditors that the bank received a poor score in the area of manuals. After three months, I presented a new manual to my supervisor that upper management later approved.

That manual became the feather in my cap paving the way to my next move—the new accounts department. It was the desk job I had had my eye on every day behind the teller line. I loved that position even more than being a teller. There, I opened new accounts and assisted new customers with our services and products. I learned about money market accounts, CDs, IRAs and other forms of investments. I thought I had died and gone to heaven. By then I had been at the bank for three years. I took bank institute classes (offered free of charge to employees) whenever they became available, including courses that would prepare me for the next job I was interested in. To say the least, I found my banking career very rewarding.

We were married three years when David and I bought our first home. It was 1,400 square feet of bliss. We first bought a small plot of land and had the house built by a local builder. It was exciting to watch our little home go up from foundation to drywall to carpet and furniture. We were living large in our two-bedroom, two-bath castle. It had a big front yard and on weekends, we loved working in it. As we planted our first maple tree in the center of the yard, we dreamed of the day that our children would climb it.

After a year of being homeowners and into our fourth year of marriage, we had our first child. We were excited new parents and the nine months couldn't go by fast enough. I enjoyed being pregnant and was able to work until the last days. During the course of my pregnancy, David and I fretted over what our son's first name would be. We narrowed it down to two names, Michael or Timothy, and decided to make the final decision on his birthday.

I had a healthy pregnancy and our beautiful baby boy was born on June 15, 1987 weighing in at six pounds and seven ounces. I'm not sure how it happened, but somewhere between the pain medication given for delivery and the pride of a new father, our son's name became David Allen. From then on, my husband, David, became "Dave" and our son, David.

My maternity leave only lasted six weeks. The first two weeks were frustrating for me, as I already felt terribly guilty knowing that I had to return to work in such a short time. I wanted to breastfeed David in those early days to give him the best, but nursing proved difficult and the doctor urged me to bottle-feed him. I cried and felt like a failure as a new mother. It was during times like these I longed for my mother's comfort and wisdom to help me through those difficult

days, but because of her alcoholism, she wasn't in any physical or mental condition to help with a newborn.

Returning to work was even more difficult. My heart
was in a tug-of-war. I wanted and needed to work, but I felt
guilty for enjoying my job and also for leaving my baby with
someone else. A family friend cared for David in her home.
David was in the best care possible but guilt still riddled me.
I didn't know how other women managed to balance career,
motherhood and marriage. I wanted to be a good mother and
be there for each of my son's "firsts."

When I went back to work and left little David with the
sitter, managing it all took more energy than I imagined. I
loved my little boy and wanted so much for him. Making a
vow to become the mother I always wanted to be required
everything in me. After an eight-hour day at the office,
I came home to care for our baby boy, prepare dinner, do
laundry and dishes, pay the bills and maintain our house.
It was exhausting, but I settled into a groove within a few
months and managed to do it all halfway well.

Banking Days

Once I was back in the routine of the bank, I was eager
to give it my best. Over the next few years, I left the new
accounts department and became the administrative assistant to the vice-president. My new boss was Mr. Brown and
working for him was my biggest challenge.

Mr. Brown was the vice-president in charge of personnel,
public relations, marketing and, most importantly, he oversaw
eight branches. He was a very intimidating man, but highly
respected. When summoned to his office, most employees
would be panic–stricken, fearing the worst. I would watch
my co-workers walk past my desk as if they were heading
to "death row." I could see the fear in their eyes wondering
if they were going to get a pink slip. Or even worse, that

he was going to ask them to do some impossible task. Mr. Brown seldom gave compliments and no one ever really knew where they stood with him. In some ways, I liked that because it made me want to work harder for him.

That position was the most rewarding for me in all eight years of working at the savings and loan, even though it took almost six months to prove to Mr. Brown my competence and my loyalty to the job. He was the type of man that when he gave an assignment, he gave few instructions, and at the same time wanted it done right. He wanted his employees to be "thinkers" and not just robots. I soon learned that his tough exterior softened once you earned his respect by showing him an action plan and the measured results of an assignment.

Eventually, Mr. Brown assigned me the responsibility of recruiting and hiring hourly employees. When the branch managers took vacations, he would send me out to cover for them. He also gave me the responsibility of the bank's advertising and marketing program. I enjoyed creating new ads and measuring their effectiveness. It was always unnerving, though, to sit across from his desk with a new ad idea. As his glasses sat perched on the end of his nose, he would study the ad and sigh. I would just sit there sweating bullets wondering what he was thinking. If the stars aligned just right in the galaxy, there was a remote chance of him liking it. And if he liked it, he'd simply say, "Good work, Krazeise! Let's run with it." That little nugget of affirmation was like winning the Nobel Prize. As Mark Twain once said, "you can live a month on a good compliment."

It took almost a year before I actually shared a laugh with Mr. Brown. He started to warm up to me and even asked about my personal interests and my family. Those few mornings when he'd ask me into his office to join him for coffee and plan the day's events were some of the best days I had in banking. Looking back to that time, Mr. Brown was one of my favorite bosses. He reminded me of the teacher everyone dreaded, but by the end of the school year, you found yourself liking.

I learned so much from him, especially how to manage the operations of a business and to bring out the best in people, and while he taught me so much, he knew his limitations and what his strengths were. I recall him once saying, "The sign of good leader is one that knows how to *look* for and *use* the talents in people and then put them in a role that best compliments them." For whatever reason, that comment always stuck with me.

Working under Mr. Brown only lasted two years. Our savings and loan was beginning to suffer financially as a result of the federal government deregulating interest rates. You may recall many savings and loans shutting down in the late '80s and early '90s. Early on, our savings and loan made a profit each year until we had to absorb a couple million dollars in losses in a short span of time. The losses were a result of the deregulated interest rates on mortgage loans and not poor management.

The government originally allowed us to take the losses over the life of the loans that the savings and loan had bought from the government. It was my understanding our savings and loan was doing well until the law changed, requiring us to absorb the loss in less time than was originally given. This was a difficult time for our bank and jobs like my position as Mr. Brown's assistant were eliminated.

From a career standpoint, this was the best thing that ever happened to me. Promoted as the retirement accounts manager, I managed a one-person department and had my own office. The only reason (and my saving grace) that I got the position was the previous bank classes I had taken. It was a great position and all of my customers were the cream of the crop. I managed their IRAs and 401(k) plans. Because of the constant tax law changes on those types of accounts,

I attended seminars often. That made for a very specialized job and offered me job security.

Back at Home

Dave was entertaining the idea of starting his own business as a Snap-on Tools dealer. His position as a collision repair manager didn't offer us much of a future and we both knew Dave was ready for more. We were nervous about starting our own business and taking this step, as it would require a big investment initially and less income coming into our household. After talking about it for weeks, we both felt it was a good move. Dave became self-employed, bought into the franchise and was assigned a territory.

Cash flow is always the biggest challenge in any new business and that meant Dave took only a small salary each week, which was a pay cut for us. Our first priority was to repay the Snap-on franchise loan that helped us start the business. It was a challenge to sell enough tools each week to repay the loan, as well as buy more inventory, build equity in the business and pay our own household expenses, but it was an exciting time, too. In the early months, I helped him stock shelves at night and input the daily receipts.

The first year of Dave's business was exciting and we were optimistic, but the zeal didn't last. After about two years of the tool business, our marriage began to show signs of stress. Our son, David, was entering preschool and our lives were full, but between managing our jobs, home and David's after-school activities, the stress began to take a toll on us. We seemed to be going in every direction and yet at the same time there was a void developing in our lives.

We were both workaholics and started to take our stress out on each other. We seldom had any time for ourselves. Dave's business had peaks and valleys and was under the constant pressure to sell more tools. The worst part was trying to collect money from some of his "dead-beat" customers that would come up with excuses to delay their payments, leaving Dave with a dwindling cash flow. It was tough building an inventory and keeping new tools on the shelf. Mechanics didn't buy tools from a catalog. They wanted to see them and hold them in their hands. So, if you wanted to sell tools, you had to have them in stock.

Signs of Trouble

By this time, Dave and I had been married eight years. We were working hard, but not on our marriage. We seldom talked and grew disconnected. We had not been in church for several years since leaving the wayward organization. Looking back, I can now see how we distanced ourselves from God and became isolated. It wasn't long after we married that we seldom spoke of the days of the Bible study group that brought us to each other and to God. Deep down, we knew that we needed to be a part of a community of believers, but we rationalized not going to church due to a busy schedule. We spent Saturdays in the yard or running errands and Sundays we just wanted to be home by the pool or grilling out.

Our marriage seemed restless and we tried our best to ignore the void. While Dave's focus was on his business, I was preoccupied with climbing the corporate ladder at the bank and other activities like the Lion's Club, Chamber of Commerce events, business meetings and David's soccer practice and games, which left little time to sustain a healthy marriage. The farther apart we got in our marriage, the more those activities filled the void. We were always on the go and yet going nowhere. We seldom had time for each other and our relationship began to look like that of roommates. The emotional connection between us had faded and the idea to recapture what we once had seemed daunting to me.

To make things worse, as an escape for Dave, he started spending a lot of time with a neighbor friend. It started out innocent, having a few beers and cheering on the Chicago Bulls during the Michael Jordan era. Before long, Dave was there every weekend and drinking more and more. I started to see a familiar pattern that made me sick to my stomach. When I made my observations known to Dave and told him I was afraid he was developing a drinking problem, he thought I was being overly sensitive and told me that I needed to "lighten up." I was overwhelmed with motherhood, my marriage and my career, and on top of it all, I had become a "nag."

I was angry with him for being so cavalier about his drinking and the resulting mess it was causing. I know that I was part of the problem because I wasn't doing much to enrich our relationship. My way of dealing with the problem was to hope it would just take care of itself. How could we ever get back on track after losing so much ground? A part of me just wanted to escape it all and end the marriage. Deep down, I didn't want to lose Dave, but I was frustrated with our empty marriage and where our lives were headed.

One evening after a heated argument with Dave, I had to attend a Lion's Club meeting. Apparently, my frustration showed on my face, because another member noticed. Pastor Tom of a local church often sat next to me at the meetings and when I walked into the room, he sensed that things weren't well. He asked me if something was wrong. That night I didn't have the energy to do what I normally do, which was to pretend that everything was okay.

"I need someone to talk to," I admitted. After the meeting, I shared with him that I thought my marriage was in trouble. Pastor Tom listened intently and said he understood. He offered to meet with Dave and me for a counseling session. On my way home that night, I knew we needed help badly and quickly. I only hoped Dave would also see the need and agree to go.

Thankfully, Dave did. Within days, we had a counseling session with Pastor Tom that lasted two hours. It was a long and quiet drive to his office, but Dave and I instantly felt comfortable with Pastor Tom as he reassured us that we were not the first or the last couple in the world to have marriage struggles. He allowed each of us to share our frustrations and point of view. And while we did not have any major conflict or issue, it was mainly a feeling of disconnection and not feeling important in each other's lives.

We were transparent about the demands of our lives and even the distance we felt toward God. Pastor Tom learned about the passion we once had for the Lord and how we first came to know God years ago. Dave was able to convey the hurt and betrayal he felt in his involvement ten years earlier with the home study group and how we had not been in Christian fellowship since.

Pastor Tom was very comforting and a great listener. He had a way of asking good questions that made us examine ourselves and re-think our priorities. Talking to him was easier than we thought it would be, especially when Pastor Tom shared that he himself had struggled with the same things in his marriage. He displayed the heart of a pastor as he cared about our relationship with each other and with God.

After he allowed Dave and me to talk, he concluded our session with one insight that put everything into perspective. "You have left your first love, that being God. In order for any marriage to survive, Christ has to be the center of it." He told us that we had let the world get in the way of our spiritual priorities. We needed to get back to God's agenda and ditch our own.

Those words were so simple and yet they cut right to the quick. We had excluded God from our lives and tried to fill that void with everything else—careers, clubs, materialism, financial success and selfish ambition. And while there is nothing wrong with having a business or career with a family, we were trying to do it by ourselves. We had fallen in the trap of defining our self-worth by what we did and not who we were in Christ.

Before we left Pastor Tom's office, we both felt a sense of healing already taking place in our marriage and in our hearts. There was a renewed hope for our future. Pastor Tom grabbed our hands, put them together and prayed over us. My heart was full and with tears running down my face, Dave squeezed my hand affirming that everything was going to be okay. During that session, our hearts softened enough to allow room for God to come in and begin healing our marriage.

After the prayer, we exchanged some light-hearted chatter about sports and the day's events. As Dave and I were leaving and thanking Pastor Tom, Dave asked if it was okay if we came to his church that Sunday. He said, "Certainly, sinners are always welcome!"

That was the one and only counseling session we ever had. The following Sunday, we found ourselves sitting in the front row of Pastor Tom's church. Like a couple of sponges, we soaked up everything that he had to say and then went home and talked about it for days. It brought back great memories of our early days together.

It took only a couple of weeks to see how far we had shifted and how misplaced our priorities had become. Looking back now, we can see how isolation from God and fellow believers made us an easy target for the enemy, who Scripture says, "is prowling like a lion looking for someone to devour." It's amazing how insidiously the enemy can seduce us and before we know it, we are out of God's will.

Our marital rift and drive for worldly success wasn't something that happened overnight. Little by little, Dave and

I had allowed the world to pull at us and weaken our spiritual roots, causing our lives to spin out of control. We made the mistake of not keeping our eyes focused on God and thinking we could direct our own lives, only to make a big mess of it all. One thing for certain is our Heavenly Father is in the business of restoring broken hearts and has the power to make all things new, including our marriage.

Dave and I recommitted ourselves to our "first love" and began attending church regularly. We made a pledge that God would reign in our lives. Finally, our marriage was growing deep roots as we grounded ourselves in Christ once again. As we examined our lives, the people around us, and the activities that consumed our time and energy, a transformation took place.

We began spending more time together and surrounded ourselves with a loving church family. For the first time in several years, we were excited and hopeful for our future together. Little did we know what an about-face our lives would ultimately undergo.

Chapter Six

The Day the Suits Came In

One Friday afternoon in 1991 around 4:45 p.m., I was at the savings and loan in my office putting some files away when two men and a woman dressed in suits walked into my office. There was an austere look on each of their faces that caused me to feel uneasy. "Are you Andrea Krazeise, the retirement accounts manager?"

"Yes," I said.

They informed me that they were agents of the federal government and, "as of 5:00 p.m. today we will be taking over this savings and loan."

"What is this, a joke?" I asked.

"Please turn over the keys to your filing cabinets," one of the men responded dryly. As I reached for my keys, he went on, "As of Monday morning, if you still want a job, you'll be answering to us." As I stood in disbelief trying to grasp what was happening, Mr. Brown came into my office and confirmed the bad news. I handed one of the men my keys and walked past them and into the bank lobby where I saw approximately 30 men and women in dark suits holding briefcases. There were guards stationed at each exit door and federal agents behind the teller line balancing out the cash drawers. Some of my co-workers were crying while guards escorted customers to the door following their transactions. It was like a scene from a movie.

By 5:15 p.m. all the employees were called in the main lobby for a briefing. A spokesman for the group read a statement informing us that the federal government was acquiring our savings and loan, and effective immediately, they were in charge. No one knew this was coming, not even the president of the bank or Mr. Brown. Shortly after the announcement, our chairman of the board arrived to explain what was happening. He was clearly shaken, as some of these agents had visited him at his office an hour before to notify him of what was taking place. Then they escorted him from his office to the bank.

My co-workers and I stood in small groups listening to the agents address a few of our questions. They told us that we could continue to work for them during the time it would take to either liquidate our savings and loan or merge it with another bank, which was a process that could take between six and eighteen months. Assuring us that no one was being fired, we were to report to work on Monday morning. As we left the building, we all had to turn in our keys. I felt helpless and confused with so many unanswered questions. On my way out, my heart broke as I saw our president's secretary clearing out his office. While she packed his personal belongings in a cardboard box the agents had provided, the president sat in his wingback chair in disbelief. It was a distressing scene and I left the bank that Friday night in a daze wishing it were just a bad dream.

On Monday morning, most of the bank's employees returned to work. We needed our jobs and we wanted answers. Plus we all figured we would have a better chance of getting a new job while we still had one. Outside the bank there was total hysteria as local news reporters were interviewing our customers. The agents forbade us to speak to the media if we wanted to stay employed. For the next two weeks, long lines of customers formed to withdraw their money. The agents prepared us to expect a rush of frightened customers. Elderly women came in confused and fearing that their life's savings were gone. We did our best to reassure them that their funds were FDIC-insured and that a new bank would be taking over. We lost about 60 percent of our deposits and the agents said that was better than they expected.

Meanwhile, employees were talking about jobs they were applying for and updating their resumes. The Feds understood our personal dilemma but could make no promises for our future. Everyday someone left for a new job at another bank. There were no hard feelings since everyone knew it wasn't their choice to leave.

Within three months, the bank across the street hired me. Mr. Brown gave me a glowing recommendation. The new bank didn't necessarily need me, but they hired me along with one of our best new account representatives and our head teller. We were the bait for the customers they wanted to lure over to their institution. At first, it almost seemed shameless of the other banks to collect the spoils of our savings and loan takeover. They figured that if they had the best employees, they would also get the desperate customers looking to deposit their money and refinance their mortgages with the familiar faces they had grown to trust. As for us, we were also desperate and needed the jobs they were offering. In many cases, the new bank paid us more to come and work for them. With each passing week, the news and drama of our savings and loan takeover seemed to fade and eventually was a distant memory.

The bank that hired me was new and offered many opportunities for advancement. Right away, management utilized my expertise in retirement accounts and they appreciated the advertising and marketing experience I brought with me. At first, there was a feeling of betrayal working for them, but to my surprise, it became a very fulfilling job. It was especially comfortable to work with some of my former co-workers. The president of the bank, Mr. Bars, was a good man and had a great "presidential" personality for the banking industry.

He was proud of how his new bank was growing and engaged with his new staff, making us all feel valued and appreciated. Mr. Bars and I had a very good working relationship. The weeks quickly turned into months of cross training as I learned different aspects of banking. There were days I was behind the teller line and others I spent behind a desk opening new accounts or taking a loan application. Since this was a smaller bank, it gave me more exposure to bank operations.

After I had been there two years, Mr. Bars called me into his office one day. He and the vice president had been meeting and as I walked in, he offered me a chair. Mr. Bars said, "We have something we'd like to talk to you about, but first, we would like for you to open this box." As he handed me the box, I thought how odd it was to get a personal gift from the president of the bank. I opened it rather nervously. What I saw inside the box brought tears to my eyes.

Enclosed was a name badge with the inscription "Andrea Krazeise, Assistant Vice-President." Under the name badge were business cards to match. Without a moment's hesitation, I leaped from my chair to shake their hands and thanked them profusely. Mr. Bars stood there smiling like a proud father as I thanked him repeatedly. He knew how hard I had worked for him and how hard I had worked at the savings and loan. In many ways, the banking business was a man's world and it always seemed I had to work twice as hard as my male counterparts to prove myself. It was without a doubt the best day of my banking career.

On that day, I became assistant vice-president of operations. That was a very big deal for me. No, it was a HUGE deal for this poor girl who had worked so hard to break free of poverty and be recognized on her own merits. I realized, too, that I could have worked another ten years at the savings and loan and never have seen that level of promotion because of the many people that outranked me in seniority and experience. Thinking back to the day the "suits" came into our savings and loan, I recall the feeling of having our dignity stripped and how the service pens we proudly wore on our lapels suddenly had no value. Everything we worked for vanished before our eyes. Then I thought back to the sixth grade when I watched my home life slowly slipping away. You realize how helpless you are in circumstances beyond your control. To receive this promotion was not only an awesome privilege, but also a personal atonement. I felt God was smiling down on me that day and granting me undeserved favor.

My Shining Moment

Weeks following my promotion as a junior officer, Mr. Bars put me to the test and asked that I make a presentation to the board of directors on a new IRA investment instrument that we wanted approved. Nervous for days, I prepared for the presentation with Mr. Bars reassuring me that I would do fine. He had great confidence in me. When the day of the meeting arrived, I waited outside the conference room until I was called. Finally, a loan officer opened the door and said, "You're on!" As I walked in, Mr. Bars poked his head out looking for Esther, his secretary to get him more coffee. She had stepped away from her desk, so he turned around and followed me back into the boardroom.

Mr. Bars sat at the end of the table and allowed me to present our proposal. At first, I was extremely nervous. Within minutes, I began to relax and feel comfortable at the big oval table among ten distinguished businessmen. In the span of 15 minutes, I made my presentation to the board. After I addressed their questions, the chairman of the board said, "Do I hear a motion to accept this...?" Ten "ayes" rang out. They approved the new investment package. As I left the room, all the men stood. The chairman said, "Well done, Mrs. Krazeise." I was so proud and walked through the door on a cloud.

As I closed the door behind me, I heard Mr. Bars say, "Oh, Andrea?" I stopped in mid-step and opened the door to see him.

"Yes, Mr. Bars?" I said with a satisfied grin.

"Could you get me another cup of coffee?" Then he looked at the other men and asked, "Does anyone else need a refill before we continue?"

My heart sank. *Did I hear him right? Did he just ask me to get him a cup of coffee?* In a split second, I felt as if a heavy blow had crushed my spirit. One minute I was an assistant vice-president confidently making a presentation before the board of directors and the next minute reduced to an entry level clerical position. Stunned, I answered with a small voice, "Sure, Mr. Bars."

I left the boardroom, rushed into the bathroom and cried. I couldn't believe what had just happened. I felt so foolish and even embarrassed for crying. Why was this simple request for coffee such a big deal to me? Was I so full of myself that I would allow serving coffee to define my self-worth? After I regained my composure, I returned with the coffee. I walked in quietly without drawing any attention to myself. They were engaged in an intense conversation so no one noticed me as I set the cup of coffee down near Mr. Bars. I left the bank and cried all the way home from the impact of a bruised ego.

It took days to lick my wounds. Finally, I took a big risk and mustered the courage to confront Mr. Bars about the humiliation I felt. I walked into his office and asked if I could have a word with him.

"Sure!" he replied cheerfully. "Are you feeling any better today?"

I explained the reason I had been so quiet the last couple of days had nothing to do with feeling sick, but something he had done. His cheerful demeanor quickly turned to a puzzled concern.

In a nervous tone, I said, "No disrespect intended, Mr. Bars. You are the president of this bank and have the authority to manage people as you see fit. I am grateful for the promotion as well as the opportunity you gave me to make that presentation to the board. I've worked hard to prove myself to you, and to have earned your respect was an incredible feat for me personally. But the moment you asked me to get you a cup of coffee…"

Before all the words came out of my mouth, he put his head down in shame and knew what he had done. He was speechless. I could tell from the look in his eyes and the way he brushed his hands across his mouth just how sorry he was.

"I am so sorry, Andrea. I never even gave it a thought. Esther had stepped away and she usually keeps my cup full. I can assure you that it will never happen again."

To my surprise, Mr. Bars was understanding and saw that this wasn't about some overzealous feminist demanding equal rights. It was much deeper than that and he understood.

Baby Number Two

Approaching our twelfth year of marriage, there were tears of joy as we were expecting our second child. By this time, David was six years old and we had been with our new church for two years. Dave and I became volunteer youth leaders and close friends with Pastor Tom and his wife and were surrounded by a great church family. This pregnancy was much different from the first one. While Mom and Dad were still drinking and living a pitiful existence, I had been adopted by a couple of older and wiser women in the church that loved me like their own and led me to a deeper under-standing of God's love for me.

My intention was to continue working at the bank throughout my pregnancy, take a two-month maternity leave and then return to work. When I informed Mr. Bars of my pregnancy, he was happy for me, but was more relieved to know that I would be returning to the bank.

Around the sixth month of pregnancy, something started to happen that I didn't expect. The desires of my heart began to change. While my baby grew inside of me, my ambition and drive for banking was becoming less and less important to me. My competitive drive to climb the corporate ladder started taking a back seat to the importance of my family life. I didn't care about it anymore. I could feel God nudging me to examine my heart and my priorities.

I wrestled with what God's will was for me and began to doubt my own plans. The idea of being a stay-at-home mom was something that Dave and I spoke of on occasion, but then usually dismissed as a luxury outside our reach. Knowing that our son, David, was entering the first grade made me realize and regret all that I had missed in his young years because of my full-time career.

The mere desire of wanting to be at home came as a surprise to me. I'll be honest and shamefully admit that for many years I looked down at women who stayed home. I thought they were a weird breed that only made us "career women" feel guilty for liking our jobs and leaving our chil-dren with a sitter. To justify my guilt, I convinced myself that they were the lazy women of our society that couldn't cut it in the real world, so they *had* to stay home. Or I thought they were wealthy women who, when they weren't eating bonbons and watching soap operas, were playing tennis at the country club and maybe doing a little charity work for kicks. Looking back, I see a very judgmental and self-righteous woman, thinking I was better than they were.

God opened my eyes to see my life from a different perspective. Having a very narrow-minded view of what it meant to be a stay-at-home mom, I witnessed several women in my church that changed the stereotype I had carried. These stay-at-home women were full of purpose and passion. They were selfless women who gladly accepted the role of being full-time moms and raising their own children, bringing back family values that many (like me) had pushed aside for money and pride.

God was calling me to recognize the value and honor of a profession that the world didn't applaud. As it appeared to so many of my friends and co-workers, staying home seemed like a luxury we couldn't afford. Truth is, maybe we could afford it. We were just too selfish and didn't want to make the sacrifice it would require. For me, it was easier to convince myself that Dave and I needed two incomes to make ends meet.

Throughout my pregnancy, Dave and I continued to talk about me being a stay-at-home mom. It seemed like a lofty idea and it was difficult to imagine not having my salary. However, we explored the crazy notion of not having my salary for the months I was pregnant and gave it a "test run." The plan was to practice by living on Dave's salary alone. We eliminated lunches out, entertainment, unnecessary shopping trips, collected coupons and examined every purchase made. During those months, we used my income to pay off as much debt as possible and build a reserve fund. We left it at that. Any decision about me going back to the bank was on hold until we sure.

Meanwhile, I went to work every day up until my due date. On November 9, 1994, I gave birth to our second son, Daniel Timothy. Dave and I, and big brother David, were crazy in love with Daniel and felt complete as a family of four. David, who was almost seven years old, bonded with his baby brother the moment he saw him. He was thrilled to no longer be an only child and made a promise to Daniel that he would be the best big brother and would always be there for him. For me, taking care of a newborn came much easier the second time around, as I was relaxed, experienced and more confident, plus I had a great support system of church friends.

After my maternity leave was over and still no clarity about me staying home, I returned to work. By this time, Dave sold the Snap-on Tools business and went back to the auto collision business. After doing the math, adding up our bills, and wrestling with the idea of not having medical insurance, it seemed we had no choice but for me to go back to work. Neither Dave nor I was happy about it.

When I returned to the bank, I was not the same woman fired up about her career and dreaming of the next challenge to conquer. Sadness hung over me like a cloud and I felt out of place. It was like I was an outsider, even to myself. What was I doing? I was determined to continue breastfeeding Daniel in those early months, even if it meant pumping during my lunch hour and breaks. I no longer volunteered to work overtime to get a project done because I wanted to be home with my children. It didn't take long to see that I wanted to take care of my children more than being at the bank.

I hated leaving Daniel in childcare knowing it would be eight to nine hours before seeing him again. By the time I got home, prepared dinner, helped David with his homework and finished bath time, I realized I had barely spent two attentive hours with my children. My life seemed like it was spinning out of control, with priorities blurred and relationships suffering. It didn't seem right. Dave noticed a change in my behavior and shared my frustrations. That went on for about three weeks.

One night, Dave was unusually quiet and I was in a somber mood. While I was preparing our dinner salads, Dave was setting the table. Daniel was in his swing napping and David was quietly playing in the other room. Sadness overcame me and out of nowhere, I burst into tears. Without my saying a word, Dave began to cry and wrapped his arms around me. God had been working on his heart as much as mine that day.

We both knew what the other was thinking and we both knew that it was time. That night, we stood in the kitchen and made the riskiest decision we had ever made. It was time to move our trust from our careers and money to trusting God and our family. After dinner, Dave offered to bathe the boys while I wrote my letter of resignation. I never felt more at peace about any decision than I did that night. After 13 years, I stepped out of the corporate rat race.

I never would have thought I would be so eager to step out of the business world, but God was doing something brand new in our lives. He was changing the way we looked at everything. Our trust grew as we began to see through God's perspective and not our own. While there is nothing wrong with being a working mom, for me, my career was my identity and I was painfully aware of that. I had always been so determined to "be someone" and prove myself to the world that I put a very important element of my life, God, in the position of being only a spectator of my life. And for so long, I tried to control my life along with everything and everyone around me. I thought I had all the answers to whatever question came along. Trusting someone other than myself was never an option for me when I was younger and yet that distrust was what I needed to surrender to Him. I never considered that maybe His plans would exceed my wildest dreams. God promises that He will guide our paths and it was time I started to follow Him down that path.

The next morning I met with Mr. Bars. After three years of working together, we had the kind of relationship that allowed me to share with him the burden I had to be home with my children. He graciously accepted my two weeks' notice, was genuinely happy for my sake and applauded my convictions. "But I am also sad to see you leave, Andrea," he voiced.

A New Season

With my banking days behind me, it took only a few months to grow accustomed to a new routine. My priority was our family and managing all the affairs of our life. From morning till night, my days filled with activities I never realized existed. Truly, it was the hardest job I ever did. Financially, things were very tight, but where there is need, there is a way. The bank allowed me to type the minutes of their board meetings at home, which took about five hours a month. I also catered the bank's board of directors meetings. I enjoyed doing this. It kept me in touch with the outside world, which I found refreshing after days of solitary confinement with a one-year-old. I also cleaned two houses a week. At times, I chuckled as I sat on my knees cleaning strangers' toilets. How silly it seemed now that serving Mr. Bars a cup of coffee had been such an emotional grenade. God taught me that humility is a wonderful thing to possess.

Those small jobs helped take the edge off the limitations set by our new budget. I liked keeping busy and with my newfound freedom, I discovered interests I never had time for, like crafts, gardening, and cooking from scratch, another money saver. I volunteered at the church, joined a ladies Bible study and was active at David's school participating in field trips. I especially enjoyed quiet moments reading to Daniel on the porch swing.

Because we lived three miles from the school, I drove David to and from school every day. This was very good for us. Over the next three years, I had a lot of time with both my sons in a minivan that held them captive to what I wanted to teach them, especially the things God was doing in our lives. I never had time for bonbons and soap operas. I guess that was all just a figment of my imagination.

Identity Crisis

I have to be honest, though. There was one difficulty I had with staying home. My career mindset had so imprinted my attitude about who I was that I sometimes asked myself, "Was being a stay-at-home mom the 'real me'?" There were moments I struggled with my identity and missed the power suits and being behind a desk, occasionally longing to make "important" decisions. The corporate rat race was challenging for me and at times I missed being in it.

Those feelings vacillated from day to day. Sometimes I felt completely fulfilled and privileged in my role at home and thought I was the luckiest woman on the planet. Other times I felt lonely, weak and unimportant, and then I felt guilty for feeling guilty. I'd ask myself, "How ungrateful can I be?" It was an institutional feeling, like someone being in a prison all her life and then set free. For so long, you knew what to expect and what was expected of you. That newfound freedom was scary at times. Since banking was all I knew most of my adult life, I had come to identify myself as a businesswoman. Now I found myself meeting new moms at the park or attending "play dates." This wasn't particularly my favorite thing to do and at times, I thought I would scream if I had to endure another conversation about sleeping schedules, breastfeeding, or ear infections.

In the past, when I met complete strangers at a gathering and they'd ask, "So, what do you do?" it was always so easy to say, "I'm a banker." To say, "I'm a stay-at-home mom" was hard. I felt like I also had to let them know that I was *once* a banker and have now *chosen* to be a stay-at-home mom, as if being home and working the hardest job in my life wasn't enough validation. But, truthfully, it wasn't enough all the time.

Thank God, those days didn't linger for long. I had good Christian friends that allowed me to vent my feelings and be completely transparent. I didn't have to wear a mask with them fearing they would reject me when I was trying to understand God's will for me. These friends saw me as a work-in-progress and helped me address my insecurities and things with which I struggled. What an encouragement they were to me. I started to understand that I didn't need to hide who I was because God made me and knew me better than I knew myself. When I began to understand how exposed I am before God, the more vulnerable and dependent on Him I became. There is no place to hide. Psalms 139 reminds me, "O LORD, you have searched me and you know me. You know when I sit and when I rise; you perceive my thoughts from afar. You discern my going out and my lying down; you are familiar with all my ways." How reassuring to know that He is familiar with all my ways, which includes the good qualities as well as the bad.

During those years of self-exploration, I soon learned the freedom of just being me. Those sweet, few years of being home full-time turned into a wonderful season of my life. As I grew spiritually, I saw my identity in Christ—not in a career, not in my role at home, not in my parent's lifestyle, or my past. My identity was the knowledge that I was His child and for that reason alone, my life had worth.

I also discovered that I didn't miss banking as much as I missed serving people. I cleaned house for a special older woman who was always grateful when I came. Cleaning her house usually took me twice as long because we would spend time talking and sharing a laugh.

There was another woman I worked for who suffered with Parkinson's disease and was unable to manage her finances on her own. Because of her shaky hands, she gladly paid me three hours a month to balance her checking account and write out her bills. She was grateful and I knew that what I was doing for her allowed her to live independently and with a sense of dignity.

The more time I spent with women like these two, the more I liked who I was becoming. God opened my eyes with these divine opportunities allowing me to be His hands and eyes. And best of all, He was using the talents and gifts that He had given me to serve others. When I look at life through His eyes, it helps me see the purpose in every season. While there is a tendency to discount certain seasons of our lives especially the times of past regrets, we could easily miss the gift in the life lesson gained. God has the amazing ability to take these seasons of our lives and prepare us for the next one.

Chapter Seven

When Nothing Changes...
Nothing Changes

The years passed with the normal routine of marriage, life and family. With my banking career behind me and staying home with our two sons, Dave and I experienced a restored faith in many facets of our lives. While on the other hand, my parents' alcoholism continued. Nothing had changed and they still lived hand-to-mouth, paycheck to paycheck, with no hope in sight. My sister, Donna, and I kept in touch and came together for holidays and special occasions at Mom and Dad's place. Donna and I were both disappointed that our children didn't have the kind of grand-parents for which we had hoped.

It wasn't easy telling the kids that Grandma and Grandpa weren't in the best condition to visit more frequently. If we wanted to catch them sober, the best days were Wednesdays and Thursdays, as they were usually broke by Tuesday night and payday wasn't until Friday. The weekends were the worst, as the beer would be flowing in abundance. Creditors continued to be a threat to their home. With no money in the bank, no telephone or car, Dad still relied on his friend, Steve, to take him to work every day to roofing jobs.

Occasionally, I stopped by their house to check on them. Most of my visits ended with me nagging them about their drinking, unaddressed health concerns, or the condition of the house. The roof leaked, the garage porch was rotting and the grass was overgrown. What concerned me most were their health issues that had gone untreated for years. Neither of them had seen a doctor in 20 years. The worst part was that they didn't seem to care. They had no desire to live a better life. To me it appeared they had checked out of life. There are no words to describe how frustrating it was to watch them live that way.

Their lives were so pathetic and depressing to me — even more than ever before once I knew the awesome power God had and what He could do for them. I wanted them to know things didn't have to be this way and God understood the despair they felt. I wanted them to know that they had children and grandchildren that loved them and wanted better for them. I wanted them to know God's love and His ability to restore their lives and give them the strength to face their fears and admit their weaknesses. I wanted so much for my mom and dad.

I pleaded with them to get help but my pleading sounded like meddling and nagging to them. I suggested that they attend a local Alcoholics Anonymous (AA) group and even offered to drive them there. Designed with 12 steps, I shared with them how the AA program could make a difference — if they were willing. But the first step was to admit they had a drinking problem and my parents remained adamant that they didn't have a problem. "If we wanted to quit, we could any time!" they said.

Rock Bottom

While I was still working at the bank, I got a phone call from my mom. It was one of those calls you fear taking,

scared to hear that one of your parents has died or developed a life-threatening health issue. The bank receptionist
called my office and said, "Your mother is on line two and
she sounds really upset." Since my parents didn't have a
phone, they seldom called me and they had never called me
at work.

I picked up the phone and before I could say anything,
Mother blurted out, "Andrea, your dad is in the hospital.
His nose has been bleeding all day and won't stop. He has
lost a lot of blood. We don't know what's wrong and you
need to come right away." I never heard my mother so
upset. I told her that I would be there within minutes. In
that moment, this confident career woman felt like a helpless child. As I drove to the hospital, I pleaded with God to
spare my father's life and allow this to be the wake-up call
my parents needed. I fervently prayed, "God, please give my
dad another chance!"

When I walked into the hospital room and saw Dad
lying on the bed in a white hospital gown, I could tell he was
scared. His face was pale and clammy. Mom sat nervously
in the chair next to him. A part of me was glad to see them
so shaken up, as I hoped it would scare both of them into
sobriety. With his nose packed tightly with gauze, he could
barely talk and had to breathe from his mouth. Within minutes
the doctor came in to speak to us. The doctor was very frank
and direct with my parents.

He told my father that the reason his nose was bleeding
was that the alcohol level in his body was causing his blood
to thin, which lessened the body's ability to form clots. The
doctor was able to cauterize the blood vessels in Dad's nose
to stop the bleeding. He made it very clear that the next time
he might not be so fortunate. If it happened again, there
was a chance the bleeding could come from Dad's throat or
esophagus. The doctor could not have been any clearer when
he said to my dad, "Sir, it would appear you have a drinking

problem and if you want to live, you need to stop. I would suggest you get some help."

"Give it to him, doctor!" were my thoughts. He said just what my parents needed to hear. I thought for certain they would finally quit drinking. But sadly, within two weeks, they were drinking again. They acted as if the nosebleed never happened. What were they thinking? I was screaming mad and in total disbelief when I went over for a visit and found them with beers in their hands. I was so frustrated and angry with them that I just yelled at them and left fuming mad.

How could they not see the severity of their alcohol addiction? They were in complete denial. What I soon learned about alcoholism is the power it has over people. The only way to save my parents was for an intervention that only God could orchestrate. Their addiction had put them on a slow suicidal course that anesthetized them even to the threat of death. I once heard another alcoholic say that "you take the first drink, after that, the drink takes you."

At the Altar

That "nosebleed" incident happened a few years before Dave and I began attending Pastor Tom's church. Later, after connecting to our new church family, I developed a close friendship with a wise and mature woman with whom I shared my parents' plight. My friend patiently listened, allowing me to be completely honest, and then prayed with me. We spoke of my parents often and on one particular day, I came to her feeling helpless and frustrated.

She gave me some advice that sounded hard to swallow at the time. "Andrea, it may be time for you to leave your parents at the altar." She explained that following her suggestion would require "letting them go." I thought, "Let them go?" Ever since I was in the sixth grade, I had watched their lives fall apart and carried the burden of thinking that somehow I had the power to fix them.

My friend lovingly convinced me that my parents were responsible for their own actions and choices. She led me to God's word in Galatians where Paul instructs us to bear each other's *burdens*, which means those heavy traumas or crises that befall each of us from time to time. But in the same chapter, Paul makes another statement that we tend to overlook: "Each man must bear his load." The word *load* is also translated as "knapsack" and each of us has a knapsack that we must carry alone. She went on to explain that in each of our knapsacks are the responsibilities, choices, feelings, pain and the past that no one but us can deal with.

In other words, love has space. While my parents desperately needed help, they needed to help themselves first. My tendency had always been to step in, take control of the situation and to fix things, with little regard to the feelings of the person I'm fixing. What finally sunk in that day was that my parents were responsible for their choices. For me to continue to offer advice or help not asked for was a lack of respect for the free-will God has given each of us, including them. Resisting the urge to fix them would require great restraint for me. My friend also helped me to see my misunderstood view of what godly strength looked liked. I thought if I was "in control" of things around me that meant I was a woman of strength.

Because of the unspoken vows I made to myself, the anger I felt at the disappointment of my parents' lives was really the by-product of my need to control. To my surprise, control masquerades as strength, but it's really not. Genuine strength looks and feels different. It has room for options. Bathed in patience, strength allows time to reflect. It also shows respect for free will. Respecting free will is a BIG concept to understand. It doesn't mean we respect the choices people make, it means we respect the freedom each of us has to make choices. I admit, I never trusted or respected my parent's choices. I mean, look at the mess they made of everything. But my friend was right. I was not their rescuer, God was. It was time for me to leave my parents at the altar and let them go.

My courage to trust Him fully in this needed to be tested. My prayers had to turn from "Please, God, sober them up" to "Lord, let Your will be done." I wanted so much more for them and now I had to accept that they had to want it more than I did. So on that day with my friend, for the first time in my life I prayed and turned my parents over to the Creator of the Universe who knew and loved them best. In my mind, I pictured me carrying my mother, and then my father, to the altar and laying them at Jesus' feet.

Not only did I leave their physical bodies there, I left their knapsacks of choices, responsibilities and their pasts at the altar. I asked God for forgiveness, as I too left my knapsack full of anger, resentment and years of bitterness toward my parents there. I also left the baggage of shame that I had carried for so long. As it turns out, my knapsack was probably the heaviest. The time had finally come for me to let go and let my Lord and Savior carry the burden for me.

As I lay them both at the altar, I turned and walked away, feeling a tremendous sense of peace. My shoulders suddenly felt lighter realizing my parents belonged to God now. As I see it, my parents always belonged to God. It just took me a long time to figure it out. For the first time, I realized the whole situation changed from that moment and it was because of the change that happened in me.

God Was Working

After I left them at the altar, my visits to my parents' house became less frequent. I came to accept the choices they were making and the fact they may never become the parents or grandparents that I wanted and longed for. I wanted so much to share my life with them and for my children to have nurturing grandparents in their lives. The harsh reality was that they may never sober up and that one day I would have to bury them like this. In some ways this was hard to take in, but on the other hand, there was a sense of freedom in knowing that I was not responsible for their lives.

Several months later, I stopped by their house for a short visit just as Dad was coming home from a long day on the roof. As Dad and Steve pulled up in the driveway, I went out to greet them. While Dad was getting out of the truck, I noticed he seemed upset. With his cooler in hand and his shirt slung over his shoulder, Dad walked straight into the house without saying a word. I walked over to the driver's side of the truck and asked Steve what was wrong. It turns out that Dad had almost fallen off the roof that day. They were working on a two-story house and Dad tripped on a bundle of shingles and lost control of his staple gun. He slid a few feet toward the edge of the roof. It was a miracle that he didn't fall off.

Dad was pretty shaken up by the incident and Steve was frustrated, too. Steve told me he felt helpless as to what he could do. Dad was a good worker and they had always worked well together. There was plenty of roofing work and Steve knew that he could count on Dad. In that backbreaking line of work, it was hard to find good help that would stick with it like Dad had done. For that reason, Steve would just overlook the occasional beer Dad had during lunch. Because he wasn't drinking hard liquor and staggeringly drunk while on the roof, Steve didn't see much harm in it—until that day.

That night I couldn't get to sleep. I tossed and turned in my bed thinking about Dad and the mishap on the roof. After a few hours, I finally got out of bed and went to the kitchen for a glass of water. As I stood at the kitchen sink,

I stared out the window. While I looked at the brilliant full moon lighting up the night sky, a thought entered my mind. A thought that I believed came from God. Had He been trying to get my attention all night? Well, now He had it, and He revealed to me one simple thing that He would have me do. I was to make a phone call to Steve the following morning and leave everything else up to God. I went back to bed and had no problem falling asleep.

Divine Plan

When I woke up the next morning, I had one assignment to fulfill. I called Steve, my dad's boss and closest friend. This was the same man for whom I babysat during the summer of the "big bucks" as a teenager. Being our closest family friend, I was able to be direct. I asked Steve if he'd be willing to set some guidelines for Dad's employment. The idea I conveyed to Steve was to consider giving Dad a choice (or an ultimatum) in order to continue working on the roof. It would require Steve explaining the risk Dad posed to himself and the company allowing him to be on the roof with a drinking problem.

I shared with Steve that he had the authority and responsibility to make attending AA meetings a condition of employment. Dad would receive a paycheck if—and only if—he could prove that he had attended these meetings. As I shared the idea with Steve, I could tell he wasn't real thrilled about the idea. He felt like he had no business telling his friend what to do. I urged Steve to think about it and to ask himself the tough question, "Had he become an enabler to my father?" Steve assured me he would consider it.

A few days later, I stopped by to see my parents. I could tell something had happened. Dad was visibly upset. When I asked what was going on, he was quick to tell me how ticked off he was at Steve. I played dumb and asked Dad why he would be angry with Steve. Dad carried on, "Steve is an SOB. He's making me to go to those stupid meetings for drunks. And if I don't go, he's going to fire me!" I maintained my composure, trying to console my furious dad. I listened with an outward compassion, but on the inside, I was forever thankful for what Steve did.

My mom was no dummy. She understood what that meant to the meager finances they had, so she made Dad go to the meetings. During the first few weeks he attended, I asked him what he thought of the meetings. He told me, "They're stupid and a waste of time." He continued drinking with abandon and at times even attended the meetings half-tanked. But he kept going and he kept his job.

It was a month later when a true miracle happened. It was in 1991 on a Friday night when Dad reluctantly attended another AA meeting and listened to a man share his personal testimony of alcohol abuse and the devastation it had caused in his life. The story the man shared was in many ways the same as Dad's. Dad later told me, "The man was telling MY story." That very night, after hearing this courageous man pour out his shame and regret, my dad made the decision to quit drinking. Just like that, he quit cold turkey. It was a day I will never forget. I was 28 years old and had been married eight years when God answered that long-awaited prayer.

Afterward, Mom got curious as to what had happened to her husband that would make him really quit drinking. So she went to a meeting with him. As Mom sat nervously waiting for the meeting to begin, a familiar woman entered the room. It was Elise, a woman who lived in their neighborhood. Mom was surprised to see her there, as they had been acquainted for many years, but she never knew Elise attended AA meetings. When Elise—who had been sober for over 30 years—saw my mother, she pointed to Mom with excitement and ran over to give her a hug. With tears in her eyes, she told my mom, "I've been waiting for you almost 20 years!"

In a very short time, Mom quit drinking, too. My parents began to attend AA meetings every night. Within a few months, they had sponsors walking beside them, encouraging them, and motivating them to stay on the road to recovery. Elise became Mom's new friend and sponsor. She played a big part in my mother's recovery. It was a perfect match and clearly evident that God had His hand on my mother and her journey to healing. Elise was a very wise Christian woman and helped Mom process her feelings and the frustrations of dealing with sobriety. Elise understood exactly what Mom was going through.

Those early months of sobriety were not easy for Mom. She was what they called a "dry drunk." Meaning she wasn't drinking, but had a lot of emotional issues to address. In many ways, sobriety was a daunting process for Mom that required facing her fears for the first time. All she ever knew was how to mask her pain with the numbness that alcohol provided. She had to learn a new way of thinking and dealing with the deep-rooted anger she had previously covered up with alcohol. She was still angry with Oma and was even angry with me. Over the years, her anger toward Oma had shifted to me, as I became the new mother in her life, hurling her with insults and shame. It was a scary time for Mom and required a lot of emotional courage and accountability from Elise. On some of those difficult days, it would have been easier to just take another drink and not deal with it all. But Mom proved faithful and worked the program with Elise by her side.

I must admit the first six months of her recovery were hard for me, too. In some ways, it was like Mom and I were on parallel paths and eventually the distance between us would narrow and meet. While she was on her path to recovery, I was on the path to learning how to trust her again, and that didn't happen overnight. It had been a very long time since I had a mother I could trust. As much as I wanted to encourage her and believe this was the new Erika, I was reluctant to exhale and trust her. I had doubts and fears that all it would take was one setback and we'd be back where we started. I wasn't entirely convinced she had the determination to stick with the program.

I soon learned that my feelings of mistrust were normal. When I'd visit Mom in those early months, I was quick to assess her speech to see if she was sober. I looked around her house for any evidence of beer cans and checked out the refrigerator. She later affirmed my apprehension and said many recovering alcoholics are familiar with what they call the *look*. It was the look I would give Mom that questioned if she was sober. It was a look that said, "Did you fall off the wagon today?" The *look* was about trust. Mom later confessed that she was very hurt by the look I gave her, but Elise had reminded Mom often about the work it would take to regain the trust she had lost over the years. Elise reassured her that eventually the look would go away, and it did.

As the months went by, she was able to be more open with me about her recovery and often shared what she was learning about herself. Forgiving herself was Mom's biggest challenge. She had to learn to accept responsibility for her actions and stop blaming others. Being transparent about her weakness made her very vulnerable. Learning to trust people — and even herself — would take time.

More than a year into her sobriety, I saw a heart of gratitude develop in my mother that never existed before. It was becoming easier for me to understand why Mom did the things she did while drinking. She taught me that alcoholism was a very selfish disease. The more I understood what the disease did to her, the easier it became to forgive her and let go of my past bitterness. I could see her being set free by a grateful spirit. She developed a joyful attitude, almost child-like at times. Mother was drawing closer to her Heavenly Father and humbled by His undeserving grace.

Never imagining that I would actually like being in her company, I found myself wanting to be around her. While God was working on her, He was working on my heart, too. Those years filled with hatred and resentment toward her melted away. There were times when I was with her that I thought I was with someone else. This new person looked like my mother on the outside, but the inside was someone new. And in time, even my mother's appearance changed and transformed into a fresher look.

Her eyes became brighter and her complexion began to glow. She treated herself to a few new outfits and a stylish haircut that boosted her confidence. Everything about her was changing, from the way she carried herself to how she wore her new eyeglasses while reading her Bible. For the first time in years, my mother started to like the person she saw in the mirror. It was wonderful to see her taking care of herself, from the inside to the outside. She had come so far.

A New Creation

As I write this, my parents have been sober for 18 years. Within the first two years of sobriety, they both received Christ as their Savior and dedicated their lives to Him. They found a loving church that embraced them. They completely surrendered their lives to God. Later, Dad was offered a maintenance job at their church, which also had a thriving Christian academy. He was thrilled about finally getting out of roofing work.

Dad's new job at the church was an incredible blessing for him. The church was a strong body of 700 believers and he was excited about being a part of it. Dad arrived early every day to set up the church and school for the services and events of the day. Praised for his faithfulness, he worked hard and loved being on staff. He took great pride in his work. The pastors and teachers came to respect his quiet strength and humble service. His ministry of service became a witness to many and earned him a promotion as head of the maintenance department with four men working under him.

With Dad's new job, which provided health insurance, they both were able to see doctors and address their medical conditions. They reconnected the phone, fixed up the house, and even got new teeth. Dad bought a car and for the first time they had money in the bank. They began giving financially to their church and did it with a heart of gratitude that was contagious. God blessed them and entrusted them with more as they proved faithful with everything they had. Their bills were paid on time and never again was their electric or water turned off.

It was amazing to watch the transformation of my parents' lives. Second Corinthians 5:17 says, "Therefore, if anyone is in Christ, he is a new creation; the old has gone, the new has come!" I was, and am still, in constant praise and amazement of how God transforms lives. To recall my parents being in complete darkness and despair, I could have never imagined this outcome. It was beyond my wildest dreams to see my parents come to this place in their lives—sober *and* following God with their whole hearts. How good it felt to finally have my parents back.

They were living in an awesome state of undeserving grace and they enthusiastically shared their faith with anyone who crossed their path. The bondage of their past was broken and gone. They were unashamed and gave all the glory to God. Never forgetting where they came from, they shared their testimony over and over, letting God use them to reach out to others who were struggling with alcoholism and other addictions.

It amazes me to this day to see how God can take the mess of our lives and use it for His glory. While Satan would like nothing more than to bind us with shame and guilt for our past, the shed blood of Jesus Christ liberates us from all our iniquities and truly covers them all. "For as high as the heavens are above the earth, so great is his love for those who fear him; as far as the east is from the west, so far has he removed our transgressions from us" (Psalms 103:11-12).

Within a few years, my parents became sponsors to others in the AA program and even chaired many of the meetings. Later Dad became the treasurer of their AA group and took care of all the finances and supplies.

The Amends

One day about three years into Mom's recovery, she called me and asked me to come over to her house. She said very little over the phone so I didn't know what to expect. When I arrived, I could tell that she had been crying. Right away I asked, "Is everything okay?" I was a little nervous about what she wanted to tell me. Was she about to tell me she had terminal cancer or something? I was eager for her to start talking and tell me what was going on. She sat down in her leather recliner and asked me to sit down on the couch beside her. In a serious soft tone she said, "I have something to tell you and I want you to be patient and not interrupt me until I have completely finished." Tears filled her eyes. What happened next will remain forever seared in my memory.

After taking a deep breath, my mother began to confess the hurt she had caused over the years. She humbly admitted to the neglect, emotional abuse and hatred she had shown me over the years and for all of this, she asked my forgiveness. She wanted me to know I was not to blame for anything and that she was taking responsibility for what she had done. I had never seen my mother so broken with regret. As she spoke, tears spilled from my eyes. I had already forgiven her years before, but whatever lingering resentment I had dissolved in an instant.

Until that day, I had never felt genuinely loved by her. For the first time that I could remember, my mother expressed her love to me. She told me that in spite of her past behavior she had always been proud of me. The unspoken pride she held for me came as a surprise.

While tears streamed down my face, I remained silent as she spoke. Extravagant mercy and grace met her heart-felt confession and request for forgiveness. My spirit was screaming with praise that God in His mercy would make my mother new as I listened to every word and waited for her to allow me to respond. In that moment, I wanted to jump off the couch and embrace her, so I did all I could to remain seated and honor her request to wait until she was finished. Sitting on the edge of the couch, wiping tears off my face, I waited and listened.

She finished by telling me how much she loved me and again asked for my forgiveness. I was already nodding my head with affirmation. Then she paused. In those seconds of silence, she looked into my eyes and as her lips quivered, she asked, "Would you do me a favor?" I remained still until she finished what she wanted to ask. She paused again and swallowed what seemed like a lump in her throat, "Andrea, I have missed so many years with you and have deprived you of so much. I want to be the kind of mother you deserve. Will you give me another chance?" I nodded with an eager yes. And she said, "Will you come over here and let me hold you?"

My mother's child stood up. In that moment, I felt like a little girl standing in front of her loving mother. As I moved toward my mother, she held out her arms for me to sit on her lap. I sat down and she nestled me in her arms. Cradled under her chin, I felt my mother's tears drip on my head as she tightly held me. Time seemed to stand still as she stroked my hair and rocked the recliner. We clung to each other and cried.

For two hours, I sat in my mother's arms. Every hug-less event in my life flashed before my eyes. As my mother hummed a lullaby and we rocked in the chair together, I felt the hug she meant to give me the day I fell off my bike and scraped my knees. I felt the hug she meant to give me the day I came home with a straight-A report card. I felt the hug she meant to give me at my sixth-grade dance recital and the hug she meant to give me the day I graduated high school. I felt the hug she meant to give me on my wedding day and the hug she meant to give me the day I gave birth to her first grandchild. I felt every hug she ever meant to give me. I felt them all…every hug.

Chapter Eight

The Calling

The days following my mother's amends were like experiencing a mountaintop view. I wanted to relive the scene over and over in my mind, as I knew I had experienced the glory of God. Her heartfelt confession was the grandeur of His grace and forgiveness. When I shared with Dave what had happened, he was just as overwhelmed as I was with the transformation that was taking place in their lives.

While God was transforming their lives, He was preparing my life for something grand also. A few years later in 1997, while attending a women's Bible study, I met the most fascinating woman. I recall meeting her years ago, but I never took the time to get to know her, as she can be somewhat intimidating. This time God nudged me closer to her in a way I never imagined. The woman I speak of is the Proverbs Woman found in the last chapter of the Book of Proverbs.

The small Bible study group that I joined had committed to studying her in an expository fashion. Each week we took a few verses and tried to determine what value this ancient woman could offer women today. We often asked ourselves, what would this woman look like today in our culture? Could we ever measure up to her and why did God give her as an example for us? Does He really expect us to follow in this superwoman's footsteps? Her life and accomplishments seem beyond our reach. However, the Proverbs Woman is more relevant than one might think at first glance.

The more I studied her, the more she intrigued me. When I examined this ideal of womanhood, I did not find a stereotypical housewife occupied with dirty dishes and laundry nor a life dictated by the demands of her husband and children. And yet, she is not a hardened, overly ambitious career woman who leaves her family to fend for itself. What I found was a strong, dignified, multitalented, caring woman who is an individual in her own right and at the same time, under the direct care and guidance of *Someone* other than herself. This savvy businesswoman has money to invest in real estate, buys and sells goods at far away markets and mentors younger women. She is her husband's partner and is completely trusted with the family's affairs and assets. This incredible woman has a heartfelt sensitivity and compassion that cares for others and fulfills the needs of people who are less fortunate. She is energetic and tackles the challenges each day brings, earning her husband and children's love and respect.

The biggest impression the Proverbs Woman made on me was the many important responsibilities she was entrusted with, and yet her first and foremost priority was looking to God. Her desire was for God's will to reign in her life. I was fascinated with her entrepreneurial spirit and her thoughtfulness to everyone around her. This was a woman who wasn't wasting her life away.

As our group studied her for weeks, a particular phrase captured my attention. Verse 13 says, "She extends her hands to the needy." Over and over, I asked myself what that meant. What does "extends her hands" look like today? As we focused on that verse, it led us to many questions. What were the needs in our community that God wanted us to pay attention to? What issues did we see in the news every day?

To whom and how would God have us extend our hands? What issue did He want us to take a stand on? We discussed various needs in the community and issues in society in which God would want us to be His hands. For me, there was one issue that kept coming to mind. It was the inescapable issue of abortion.

I don't know why the topic of abortion kept entering my mind. I wanted that subject to move aside in my thoughts as I tried to think of other ones less controversial. As we went around in the group, we each shared the thing that God had put on our hearts. When my turn came, I wanted to share the burden of homelessness or battered women, but instead the word "abortion" came from my lips.

I always knew in my heart that abortion was wrong in God's eyes. But for the most part, I was pretty lukewarm on the issue. Truth be known, I never gave it much thought until that day. I mean, what could I do? It's a woman's choice, isn't it? Besides that, abortion is controversial. Why would I want to get involved in a heated battle like that when I was comfortable on the fence balking at the overzealous Christians picketing abortion clinics?

As we closed our Bible study that night, we prayed about what God had laid on our hearts. Our assignment for the following week was to research the issue and ask God what He would have us do. I recall having a half-hearted prayer about it, thinking my "issue" would eventually pass. I thought, *why couldn't I get recycling plastics, serving at a soup kitchen, or teaching literacy to after-school kids?* The issue of abortion seemed too big and I wasn't sure I wanted to take it on. However, I knew that the group would hold me accountable to share my findings at the next meeting and I didn't want to show up empty-handed, so I did a little research.

My Eyes Were Opened

Within a few weeks, my "little" research turned into me becoming a lay expert on the issue of abortion. I studied abortion online and from books, eager to learn everything I could about abortion procedures, the medical consequences, statistics and the emotional impact abortion had on women. I visited crisis pregnancy centers, the Florida Right to Life office, spoke to area doctors and even called abortion clinics. To my surprise, I developed an insatiable appetite for information on the subject, which for some reason I couldn't get enough.

The reality of abortion and the devastating consequences it had on a mother and her baby shocked me. Deeply impacted by what I learned, I wanted to hear from women who had experienced an abortion and find out what their feelings were. It was heartbreaking to discover the crippling effects it had on women emotionally. When I studied fetal development, I saw for the first time the horror of abortion and the graphic nature of what we call "choice." The numbers were so great and the implications of my guilt were disturbing.

I was disappointed in myself, knowing for so long I had been lukewarm on abortion and had never taken the issue seriously. I thought how blindly ignorant I was not to see this tragedy around me. I could only imagine how it must look through God's eyes. My heart became inflamed. There had to be something I could do, but I didn't know what. I began to pray, *"Lord, if this is your will, make it clear to me. Send me a sign or something to tell me that you want me to get involved."*

Face to Face With Evil

As I did my homework, I called abortion clinics often and spoke to various nurses and schedulers that would take my calls. When I asked about specifics of the procedures, they gave me very little information. It was only when I persisted that I got a few more facts, but not many. They preyed on a woman's fear and offered nothing but a price quote and appointment time. I remember one occasion when I inquired about a late-term abortion, as the state of Florida allowed abortions up to 28 weeks. When I asked the nurse how the procedure was performed on a 24-week pregnancy, she explained in a very matter-of-fact tone, "the procedure involves a vaginal delivery of a stillborn." I couldn't believe what I was hearing. Trying not to sound shocked, I asked her how the fetus becomes a stillborn. She stated, "The medication injected into the amniotic fluid stops the heartbeat of the fetus."

She went on to explain, "Following that medication, another drug would be administered to start the contractions to deliver a stillborn." Never did they refer to the fetus as a baby. Moreover, they never asked if I had considered other options first. To the abortion clinics, the procedure was an easy solution for the right price. Getting straight facts from them did not come easy.

"What about giving them the truth and some other options?" I asked them. "Do you tell the women about the development of their baby or emotional trauma they may face as a result of an abortion?" Their genuine concern for the young women seemed unimportant, as they stressed the relief one would feel when the abortion was over. They figured the less she knew the better. I was furious. What an insult to women! And to think abortion clinics are pro-choice. If they were truly pro-choice, they would have enough respect for women to help them make an informed choice. It's only when a woman knows the truth and all her options, that she can make an informed decision. I was outraged with the thought of thousands of young girls entering those doors blindly each day. They deserved better.

During my research, the greatest impact was learning that 95 percent of post-abortive women would not have ended their pregnancy had they known that someone was there with options. For these women, to know that they were not alone and hear the truth about their unborn child might have changed everything for them—and that truth didn't have to come from a doctor or pastor. That person could be anyone, like you or me.

The number of suffering post-abortive women was staggering. It was daunting to think about the number of women in my own community and even in the church who carried regret over an abortion. My heart became especially heavy for post-abortive women living in their private hell of shame and guilt, emotionally scarred for years after their own abortion experience. There was so much I wanted to tell them about God's love and forgiveness—that He would forgive them and help them become whole again. Healing and wholeness was a great need in the pro-life movement. The implications of knowing there were so many hurting women was overwhelming. There were times I had to stop what I was doing and pray for them, for women I did not know, but knew existed.

One day I was driving to our Bible study and I heard Dr. James Dobson (from Focus on the Family) on the radio telling a story about the holocaust. He described a little church in Germany in the 1940s that stood near a railroad track. Occasionally during Sunday services, a train would pass by filled with men, women and children. Everyone in the church knew the train was headed to the concentration camps, but like so many of us, they thought, "what can we do?" When the sound of a distant train approached, the pastor would turn to the choir and say, "Let's just sing a little louder," hoping to drown out the screeching sounds of the passing train. Dr. Dobson went on to explain the similarities of the holocaust during World War II and the holocaust of abortion.

He said, "While those church people all knew what was going on, they sat and did nothing. They were too afraid of persecution, just like we are about taking a stand against abortion. But what would God have us do...sing a little louder?" Dr. Dobson's words pierced my heart and that was all I needed to hear. As tears rolled down my face, I knew God was calling me to be His hands and eyes for the unborn. I didn't want to be a Christian who just "sang a little louder" as precious lives were heading for destruction. That story was the sign for which I had prayed.

The abortion statistics were staggering. Every 20 seconds an abortion occurs in the United States. That's 4,600 abortions a day, 150,000 each day worldwide. I saw graphic images of dismembered baby bodies and it was horrifying. I never could have imagined such a nightmarish scene. As I viewed those images, I wondered what Jesus must feel. Knowing that God is everywhere at all times means He is present at every abortion procedure performed, grieving at every life that He created destroyed in the name of choice.

It became easy to lose myself in deep thought and anguish over this issue, one that I had never before given a second thought. It wasn't until one night before I fell asleep that God gave me a glimpse of His sadness over all the babies that were dying and the women who would forever mourn. This glimpse, or "vision," didn't come in some over-spiritual way that would make me believe I was the "chosen one" to stand against abortion.

I believe He gave me this vision to awaken what He wants us ALL to see—that abortion is the greatest moral evil of our time. It carries the same too-horrifying-to-be-true specter the holocaust had on the previous generation. Experiencing God in a deeper way than ever before, I was starting to see things differently—and more importantly—through His eyes.

From God's Perspective

One night, after I had gotten the boys tucked in, I lay in bed restless and unable to fall asleep. The past weeks I had learned so much and had often been in deep thought trying to comprehend it all. As I lay there thinking and praying, I started to imagine what God sees. I got to thinking how a satellite camera zooms in from outer space. First, I saw the image of the entire planet Earth appear and then the image zoomed closer to the North American continent and then continued to zoom closer to the United States. The scene zeroed in to my state, then to my town and then to dozens of houses in nearby neighborhoods.

God, whose ability is far beyond any satellite camera, can penetrate the walls and see into the bedroom of a young girl crying, knowing that the next morning she would walk through the doors of an abortion clinic. And while He watches this young girl in America during the dark of night, on the other side of the world, in the daylight, He can see thousands of girls at abortion clinics, each of them laying on cold examining tables while their tiny wombs are being violated in ways He never intended.

As God witnesses each abortion, His heart grieves for every child He made in His image. He had a perfect plan for each one of them until their mother's free will became their worst enemy. He wanted to be there for that frightened young girl, but sadly, she did not know her Creator and the promises He had for her. No one ever told her about His love and that He had a better plan for her and her baby. With His omnipresent and omniscient power, while He watches these young girls on the examining tables, He sees the young men sitting in the lobbies of the clinics. Gripped by fear, they sit wringing their hands, wishing they were anywhere else but there.

While God watches hundreds of doctors perform one abortion after another, He hears their thoughts as they convince themselves they are providing a service desperately needed. God sees the nurses, the receptionists and the appointment schedulers in the abortion clinics all busy at their work, eager to schedule an abortion, hoping it helps justify their own pro-choice position. God's heart grieves for them all—the pregnant girl, the young father, the doctor, the nurse, and most of all, the unborn child who is undeniably the weakest. It is sad to think of how many people are involved in ending one defenseless life. The thought of God watching this every day, 150,000 times a day across the globe is heartbreaking.

This vision played out like a movie for several nights. God was rattling me for sure. I lay there thinking, "God, what would You have me do? I am but one person." During those long nights of deep thought, I would lie in bed knowing at that very moment there was a woman on the other side of the earth walking through the doors of an abortion clinic, her and her unborn baby. Within hours, she would walk out, but this time alone. I recall thinking maybe if I prayed that very moment on behalf of someone I didn't know, maybe she would change her mind, as some occasionally do. I believed in the power of prayer, so I prayed that God would intervene and save her child from the grips of the enemy.

Within days, I finally surrendered to God's calling on my heart. It was then that He poured a liquid fire in me—part passion and part fury. I eventually stopped asking the question "What am I to do?" and found myself on the front lines in the war against abortion. Unclear exactly what I was going to do, I knew making a difference on abortion meant ministering to one woman at a time. He commissioned me to seek these women and to speak the truth in love and then to back it up with action. "Let us not love with words or tongue but with actions and in truth" (1 John 3:18). And even though my heart's desire was for every woman to give life to her unborn child, I was mindful of her own free will. I would respect her free will, even if I didn't agree with her decision.

Equipped to Serve

My commission began by volunteering on an "abortion information" hotline in the Orlando area. The hotline was available for abortion-vulnerable women to call in requesting abortion information. Trained lay counselors manned the hotline. Within a month I became one of those trained lay counselors helping reduce women's anxiety and directing them to a crisis pregnancy center in their area where they would receive a free pregnancy test and confidential counseling. The hotline calls were directly transferred to my home phone during my shift hours. Being a stay-at-home mom, I could easily man the phone without leaving the house.

My shift was from Sunday night to Monday night. I took this responsibility very seriously. Covering the kitchen table was my counseling manual, notes for common questions asked, a map of Central Florida and the location and operating hours of area crisis pregnancy centers. In the course of my shift, I typically received 10 to 15 calls. Soon I added another shift so I could talk to more women. Before each shift, I prayed that my words would be His and that He would use me in spite of my inadequacies.

"Lord, please keep me calm while each caller explains her plight. Help me be Your ears and voice of compassion to her." After each shift, I prayed for every woman I spoke to and turned each one over to God. "Lord, thank you for loving these women more than I can ever imagine and for using the words You spoke through me to help them through this crisis." Letting the clients go is an essential part of counseling, as it is easy to doubt yourself or feel you let the client down.

Over the next few months, I received many calls from abortion-minded women and God gave me the privilege to minister to them. However, it didn't take long to figure out that there was something very important missing. Every time I directed a young woman to a crisis pregnancy center, I became painfully aware that there wasn't a center in my own town. Too often, I found myself directing women from my area to crisis pregnancy centers (CPCs) in the next county. With every call I took, the realization of the need grew clearer. As I talked with the other hotline counselors, they all agreed that *someone* needed to start a CPC in Sanford.

Chapter Nine

Cherish the Fear

Months passed while I served on the hotline and I was reminded frequently of the need for a CPC in our area. I wrestled with the thought of starting a CPC in Sanford and made all kinds of excuses why God couldn't possibly be calling me to the task. I was the least qualified; surely He had someone else in mind. Yes, I knew the statistics. Yes, I felt the burden for women. Yes, I was a trained phone counselor. And yes, I wanted to help. However, that doesn't qualify someone to start a non-profit organization.

I shared my burden with an area pastor and friend, Jeff Krall. As it turns out, he and some other pastors had been praying for someone to "rise up" and start a CPC in our town. Pastor Jeff had been waiting for someone like me to answer his prayer. As I shared the idea with him, I also shared my fears. Pastor Jeff reassured me that God wouldn't put this kind of burden on my heart without also making a way to provide for all that would be needed—including making up for any inadequacies on my part. Pastor Jeff then said something that has stuck in my mind to this day. He said, "God doesn't call the qualified. He qualifies the called."

Days following that meeting with Pastor Jeff, Dave and I took our boys on a family vacation to the mountains. It was a wonderful opportunity for me to spend time in reflection and soul searching. The words Pastor Jeff spoke to me replayed over and over in my mind. As I shared all these thoughts with Dave—about this burden that the Lord was putting on my heart and how I felt led to do something more than serve on the hotline, he was very supportive and encouraged me to seek God's will. After many conversations with Dave—and God—on the front porch of that mountain cabin, I felt it was unmistakably clear that God was preparing me for something big. The only thing that felt right was to accept the challenge of starting a crisis pregnancy center in Sanford, Florida.

My soul danced at the thought of how God could use a CPC to save women and their babies from abortion in my city as well as heal the hearts of countless women from post-abortive heartache. I felt such an excitement and passion. However, my emotions wavered from a spirit of peace at the thought of what could be accomplished to a spirit of fear when the reality set in.

Could I really do this? I only knew a little about getting a business started from when Dave started his tool business years earlier and my experience at the bank. A non-profit organization was uncharted territory for me, which allowed self-doubt to strengthen its grip. Who was I to think I could pull that off with no experience? How could I start a crisis pregnancy center and counsel women into making life-affirming decisions? Who was I to do that?

Then out of the blue one day, my husband spoke three memorable words to me. When I was struggling with self-doubts, Dave said to me, "Cherish the fear." He explained, "no one should ever be so confident that they think they can do anything by themselves." Dave was right. When I am completely dependent on the Lord, the fear reminds me that I need Him to walk me through the process.

Days later, I was reading the Bible and came across Proverbs 16:3-4, "Commit to the Lord whatever you do, and your plans will succeed. The Lord works out everything for his own ends." It was then I realized that God would figure this all out for me. I had a completely new perspective. Not that everything was going to be easy, but I had an assurance that God would guide me every step of the way. God would be in charge and He had an agenda in which I was going to play a vital role. That was a liberating feeling. I rested in the truth that He would supply all my needs. When I ran low on strength, courage or energy, I knew God would give me more, and give it in abundance.

The concept that God would reveal wisdom and truth in meeting the needs of these women was a spiritual hurdle that He had to prove repeatedly. When I lacked understanding or direction, I relied on the only thing I knew for sure, and that was the promise found in Proverbs—He "works out every-thing." I knew that God can do anything and He can do all things through me because Christ dwells in me. These truths kept my passion alive and my eyes fixed on Him.

I soon realized I had stepped into the bargain of a life-time. (And believe me, I love a good bargain!) Not only had God called me into ministry, He was also asking if I would go into business *with* Him—not just *for* Him. He had the busi-ness plan, the capital, the strategy, and knew the outcome right from the start. I knew He would share it all with me in His perfect timing. All I had to do was show up every day with a teachable heart and ask, *"What are we going to do today, Lord?"*

I knew I'd be a fool to turn down such an assignment. So I began every day by talking to God just like He was sitting at my table having a cup of coffee with me. *"What's on our agenda, Lord? Show me what to do today. Open the doors that You would have me walk through. Close the ones I don't need to bother with. Put people in my path that will partner with me and walk with me in ways that would honor You. Help me stay focused on You. Please keep the enemy out of this—or at least help me recognize his traps early in the journey. Help me understand the spiritual fight into which I am entering. Have Your way today."* I knew Satan hated that God was going to use me to save women and babies from his seductive lie that abortion was their only answer. I knew that he comes for only three reasons—to steal, kill, and destroy, and those three verbs describe abortion.

In August 1997, the first Sunday after we returned from our mountain vacation, I went forward at the end of our church service to accept the call to pro-life ministry. I had talked to friends, family and elders of my church when we got home and they all gave me their blessings.

Within a month of announcing the vision to open a crisis pregnancy center in Sanford, Pastor Jeff invited me to his church one Sunday to share with his congregation what God had put on my heart. He and his church embraced the vision. Following the service, they prayed a blessing over me and commissioned me into the ministry. Pastor Jeff Krall of Family Worship Center in Sanford was one of my champions from the very start. Wise advice seemed to flow from God's heart to Pastor Jeff, as he had a special way of empowering me with courage and reminding me who I was because of Him.

After that incredible prayer, Pastor Jeff asked if there was anything specific that he and the church could do for the future center. I suggested that they continue to pray for supporters and volunteers. He applauded that, but suggested that we also focus on finding a building for the center. At that point in time, I hadn't begun to think that far ahead or that BIG. Pastor Jeff was way ahead of me.

He said to his congregation, "Let's pray that God would send the center a building and let's ask that it would come as a gift." I remember thinking, *"A gift...as in 'free'?"* My faith couldn't wrap itself around the idea of a building at no cost. *"Okay, Pastor Jeff, whatever you say! Let's pray!"* Following the service, Pastor Jeff presented me with a $1,000 check. What a break that was. It was the exact amount necessary to file our corporate and tax-exempt application with the state of Florida.

Within a few weeks, I recruited some friends and we had our first organizational meeting at my house. Our steering committee included 12 of us—me, Dave, my dad, Lisa Winstead, Tony Warren, Deanne Warren, Bev Koegler, Paul Koegler, Laurie Wren, Del Marie Howell, Kathy Holley, and Celeste Pipitone. There was no question in our minds that evening, we had a huge task ahead that would take a great deal of physical, emotional, and spiritual stamina. The first line of business was to name the future center and set an opening date. The "Sanford Crisis Pregnancy Center" would open its doors on June 1 of the following year. That gave us ten months to make the vision come to life.

We tackled the easy and practical things first. We formed a corporation, filed for tax-exempt status and began hitting the pavement to recruit churches, organizations and individual donors to stand behind our vision. As we developed a business plan, we began to build a library of educational material and brochures that would one day serve as tools when counseling our clients.

It sounds crazy now as I look back on what happened during those early days. We were asking churches to stand behind something that didn't exist. We approached them with an expectation that they would support a vision they could not yet see. Sanford's new CPC existed only on paper. As our steering committee members shared, talked, prayed and painted visual pictures to potential partners, results came slowly. When we lacked confidence that strangers would stand with us in our efforts and when all we could do was stand on the Lord's promise and wait, He would open the most resistant doors and pour out blessings and favor. Those were exciting times.

Cheerleaders

One of the steering committee members, Celeste, wanted me to meet a priest who was a friend of hers to share the vision of our center with him. Father Trout was like a shot of high energy with a "Go get 'em, girl!" attitude. It was amazing how that meeting began and ended. It felt like Father Trout was waiting for us to walk into his office that day and tell him about our new venture. Like God had already met with him and said, *"Now listen up, my faithful servant! Andrea and Celeste are on their way here to meet you. Andrea will be a little nervous, as you are the first church she'll approach. So be easy on her, give her your support, and back it up with a $500 check."* Within 15 minutes of meeting with him and after a few questions, Father Trout gave us his blessings and sent us off to "get to work" with a $500 check.

The best part of meeting Father Trout was later realizing how God used him to introduce me to someone who would become not only my biggest cheerleader, but also my "Apostle Paul." As the idea of the CPC started to take shape, we all saw the tapestry of people God was using to accomplish this task. I recall asking God to send me two people in particular to help me along the journey. His word says in 1 John 5:14, "This is the confidence we have in approaching God: that if we ask anything according to his will, he hears us."

I had so many questions about the pro-life arena and things I didn't understand. I wanted wise counsel from people who had direct involvement with both sides of the issue—someone informed of the pro-life movement and someone informed of the abortion business. Knowing my limitations and that there was so much I needed to learn, I specifically asked for *my own* Apostle Paul to assist me just as the real Apostle Paul in the Bible had assisted the young preacher, Timothy. I longed for someone who had experience in the pro-life movement who could teach me and take me under his wings.

Sadly, the media has never depicted pro-life work in a positive light. As soon as I told some folks I was getting involved with pro-life work, they'd often say, "Are you going to be one of those people that stand in front of abortion clinics yelling at women showing graphic pictures of aborted babies?" I knew God wasn't calling me to do that and that was a stereotype I wanted to overcome. There are many facets of pro-life work aside from sidewalk picketing. The truth is, there aren't many radical pro-lifers who yell on the sidewalks and show graphic images anymore, for which I am grateful. Extreme tactics may have existed in the early days of Roe v. Wade, but today the focus is on the mother and how we can extend a helping hand and the love of Christ to her. I'm sad to say that the negative image of pro-lifers was the stereotype I held, too, and people need to be re-educated about the positive side of pro-life work. There was so much to learn about how to do pro-life work effectively and what I needed was someone to show this little "Timothy" the way.

During the meeting with Father Trout, he spoke of a man named Dr. Al who was entering the seminary and would be in town within the next couple of weeks. Father Trout described Dr. Al as an active pro-lifer who had devoted his life to saving lives. Dr. Al had been a cardiologist by profession for 50 years and was now retired. Dr. Al and his wife had eight children and she had died 12 years earlier. Dr. Al heard God calling him into the priesthood at the age of 75. I was fascinated by what Father Trout had to say about him, until he told me that Dr. Al had been arrested 45 times as a result of laying his body in front of the doors of abortion clinics.

"What? Arrested 45 times? Did I hear that right?" My jaw dropped when I heard that. While he certainly sounded interesting, I wasn't sure I was ready for someone that "radical." Father Trout could see my shocked surprise and assured me that Dr. Al was someone I would want to meet. I wanted to believe Father Trout, as he had a great reputation in our town and I trusted he wouldn't connect us with some "loose cannon."

Within weeks, I got a phone call from Dr. Al. He had just arrived in town and been briefed by Father Trout about what our steering committee was doing. "I would like to hear more about your vision of starting a crisis pregnancy center. Is it possible we can meet?" Dr. Al asked. It just so happened we were having a meeting that night at my house, so I invited him to attend. When I opened the door to meet him, I knew right away that I liked him. Dr. Al was a thin man with a kind smile. He was soft spoken and had a gentle spirit. My first thought was, *"There's no way that this is the rebel with a rap sheet of 45 arrests!"*

During the meeting, Dr. Al listened attentively and took notes. Much of what I shared that night included my findings of the other CPCs in neighboring counties that I had visited. I shared some operational procedures, and a list of educational materials in which we needed to invest. I also shared the success rate of CPCs in leading abortion-vulnerable clients to life-affirming decisions. Our small group was excited about the future and eager for our next step. As we closed the meeting, I challenged all the members to begin seeking location sites for our future center. I suggested, "Let's keep our eyes open and look around mini-malls or for affordable office space we could rent." Since we didn't have much money, leasing a space seemed like the best route to take.

Dr. Al sat quietly. I asked him what he thought of our plans or if he would like to share anything. He said that he was very impressed. Then he humbly shared with us how he had been involved in pro-life work for years and arrested numerous times. "However," he added, "in all my years as a protestor I am not convinced that I saved one baby. What you are doing with this future center sounds like a more effective way to reach those women and save their babies. If you will have me, I would like to join in your efforts."

"Count yourself in, Dr. Al!" The words slipped out before I could stop them, but I am so glad they did. He became our most active member. Because of his M.D. credentials, many doors opened and our vision picked up speed. In those early months, Dr. Al and I spent a lot of time together making plans, recruiting new donors, screening volunteers and organizing a training workshop. He was a bundle of passion and wisdom and I loved being with him. Dr. Al became the Apostle Paul for whom I had prayed. He taught me so much about the pro-life movement and every time we met, he had a new stack of pro-life articles or materials for me to read. He was as excited about the center as I was. I never would have imagined my Apostle Paul being a 75-year-old man with a record of 45 arrests. Now that I think about it, wasn't Paul arrested and imprisoned many times as well?

My "Centurion Soldier"

Another person I prayed for was someone who had once worked in an abortion clinic and later crossed over to the pro-life side. Then I learned of a group called the Society of Centurions. They were former providers of abortion who had abandoned that practice and now embrace the sanctity of life. Their number included physicians, nurses, receptionists and anyone involved in the abortion business.

They called themselves "centurions" in honor of the centurion soldier who stood at the foot of the Cross of Christ and became horrified at the crucifixion in which he had taken part. When Christ died, this centurion dropped his sword and fell to his knees exclaiming, "Surely, this was an innocent man!" Those who participated in aborting unborn children are the centurions of today. They have dropped their swords against the unborn and now recognize the depth of their guilt and desire healing and reconciliation.

Many of these folks were rescued by Christians who had been praying for them for years. Now their conversions were making incredible headways in the pro-life work and for the Kingdom. I wanted to partner with someone who knew the truth and could validate what really goes on in the abortion clinic and who could help me understand the client's state of mind in this situation. I wanted to learn how we could better reach the abortion-minded women in our midst. I figured it was like knowing the opponent's plays and it certainly would help to know the enemy's game plans.

God provided that centurion soldier in my good friend, Laurie Wren. I learned of Laurie when I met her pastor at a ministerial group to which Pastor Jeff had invited me to speak. Following my speech, her pastor was quick to tell me of someone I would be fascinated to meet. He described Laurie as having a burden for post-abortive women. Without hesitation, I called Laurie that evening. Her pastor was right—she was fascinating and we talked for two hours, each sharing our burdens.

Laurie worked as a counselor at an abortion clinic some 15 years earlier and now was a devoted believer of Jesus committed to saving the lives of the unborn and their mothers from the consequences of abortion. Laurie allowed me to ask questions about the abortion business and her role in the abortion clinic where she once worked. She answered questions I could never ask the clinics I called. Her honesty and straightforward answers validated the evil I had only read about. Talking to Laurie confirmed the calling God was putting on my heart. I no longer doubted if some of what I had learned was just over-sensationalized rhetoric.

Laurie was excited to hear the plans to start a crisis pregnancy center. She was eager to be a part of the process and within weeks became my faithful co-laborer and sidekick. What I came to admire most about Laurie was her humility and the confidence she had knowing that it was by the grace of God she had been forgiven and given new life. She saw the pain from her tragic experience as a gift from God preparing her for the ministry He was calling her to. Her heart went out for the women who have suffered an abortion. Laurie's passion was to lead brokenhearted women to Jesus where He would meet them with healing and freedom.

Laurie's friendship and partnership was a gift to me. Her tender spirit and enthusiasm for our future ministry was just what I needed. Months following our first encounter, she shared a very personal story with me (and granted me permission to share with you). I asked Laurie one day what was the rock-bottom event that led her to leave the abortion business. She told me that her primary role at the clinic was to counsel the clients and basically reassure them they were making the right choice. On occasion, the abortionist asked her to accompany an emotional client during the abortion procedure. She would stand beside the frightened woman holding her hand and attempt to keep her calm and still during the procedure.

Each day, a staff member at the clinic would carry a large heavy-duty trash bag out to the dumpster in the parking lot. The bag contained the remains of aborted babies. One day the clinic was short-staffed and that task fell to Laurie. That was the moment when she was struck with the reality of it all. Tears rolled down her cheeks as she confessed and shared these words with me, "The tiny arms, tiny legs…quenched before awakened. They never had a chance. Now they would be put in the trash—no ceremony, no recognition. I thought of all the lives that the trash held. One may have been a talented musician, one may have been a scientist who would have discovered a cure for cancer, one may have had a radiant, encompassing smile, one may have been a loving foster parent, and one may have been your child's best friend. We may never know who they were, who they might have become, but one thing is certain—THEY WERE!"

Laurie was right. Some may call them "fetal tissue" or any other detaching terminology, but the truth remains, they weren't potential human beings, they were human beings with potential.

The Vision Gets an Address

Two months into our partnership, Dr. Al called to tell me about a possible site location for the center. He was overly excited about his find and insisted that I meet him at the designated address in an hour. I had a general idea of the area, but couldn't picture the mini-mall or office space of which he was speaking. When I arrived at the location, I saw an old house that sat on the main drag of our town. Once it had been a quaint cottage and later, a Greyhound bus station, but now it was nothing more than a ramshackle little building.

The bigger problem was that it was for sale. Dr. Al couldn't have meant this location. I thought maybe he meant for me to go across the street because there was a mini-mall with two little offices.

I was at the correct address, but it didn't make sense. Within minutes, a real estate agent showed up and asked if I was Andrea. I nodded. The agent then asked, "Well, what do you think?"

I was more than a little confused. "What do you mean, what do I think? I think there must be some mistake. Is this building for rent or for sale?"

He said, "It's for sale for $86,000 and Dr. Al wants you to take a look at it."

I shook my head and said, "I think there is a serious misunderstanding. We're not in a position to buy this building."

The agent said, "Why don't you go in and take a look while we wait for Dr. Al?"

At that point I was a little aggravated, but I didn't want to stand there arguing with him until Dr. Al arrived. So I went into the cottage and looked at it. It was a mess. My first thoughts were how pathetic it was. The walls had wallpaper falling off with lattice trim nailed to the bottom half of the walls. Light bulbs were hanging on strings. Mildew stains covered the sinks and toilets. I spotted two dead birds that apparently got trapped inside after coming in through the chimney. The carpet was old and stained. The tile was all cracked and broken up. The place smelled really bad and the floors were uneven. The building was probably over 60 years old and to say the least, the place was a real rat hole. I found it impossible to think that they had the nerve to ask $86,000 for it. The only good thing I could see about it was that it was in a great location and had plenty of parking.

Suddenly, I heard voices outside. I figured Dr. Al had arrived and went out to meet him. Dr. Al cheerfully approached me and asked, "Well, what do you think?" I was stunned and didn't know where to start. I looked at the agent and asked if I could speak to Dr. Al privately. He kindly backed away from us.

With a disgruntled tone, I said, "Dr. Al, I don't mean to hurt your feelings, but I think we've had some kind of major communication problem. We are not in a position to buy this or any building. They want $86,000 and we have only $300 in the bank. Our plans were to find a cheap office to rent. I don't want to waste this guy's time...."

In mid-sentence, Dr. Al stopped me. "I understand. But why don't you go look inside again and tell me what you *really* think. Tell me if you think the building has potential. Go ahead, go look and come back." Being scooted away like a child, I took a deep breath and decided that time would be best served to appease him and just go back in. I would look again, exit quickly, and tell him the same thing—and some more.

In a quiet huff I walked past the agent and went inside the building. I could hear them talking outside and that made me a little nervous. Silently I prayed, *"Please, Dr. Al, don't commit us to anything!"*

I entered the front door. But this time, something supernatural happened. It was as if God took off my glasses and put His glasses on me when I walked in. A transformation took place right before my eyes. When I looked at the front room, I saw clients sitting in white wicker furniture. The room was bright and there were lots of windows with plenty of sunshine streaming in. I went to the next room and I saw an office with three workstations. I saw myself on the phone and volunteers filling out intake forms.

I walked down the hall and came across two more rooms. One had a cozy fireplace. I felt like I was in a time warp because I had just been there and seen dirt, filth, dead birds and years of neglect. Now I was envisioning comfortable furniture, lamps, and a client and counselor talking together. I continued down the hall and came to two bathrooms. One bath was set up to be a lab and the other was for clients. The house was showing signs of potential.

Next I could see a bright room filled with books, resources and baby models that were available for counselors to educate clients. It held all our educational material and there were even brochures stacked up on shelves. Then there was a quaint little kitchen and a huge walk-in closet that housed our little boutique. Baby clothes hung on racks and shelves were stocked with diapers, wipes, blankets and bottles. The old place had lots of potential and I could see it being a great place for a crisis pregnancy center. The idea of restoring the old building was starting to sound pretty fun. Maybe Dr. Al's idea isn't as crazy as I first thought.

Then in a snap I came back to reality. *"Andrea, what are you thinking? You can't afford this. You have only 300 measly dollars in the bank!"* My joy evaporated as clarity returned. I went back outside to talk to Dr. Al and try to bring him back to reality as well.

"Well, Andrea, does this place have potential?" he asked rubbing his hands together with a big smile. "Don't you think it would be perfect with a little bit of help?" He was so happy to have found this place. It was heartbreaking to have to burst his bubble.

"Dr. Al, remember what we talked about? We were going to rent and just have an office and…we can't afford to put ourselves into debt."

Before I could finish my lecture, he interrupted me, "Yes, but do you think this building would work for you?"

Why couldn't he understand? "Dr. Al, one of us is not making sense today. Is it you or is it me?"

"Andrea, would this building work as the Crisis Pregnancy Center for Sanford, Florida?"

"Yes, I think it would work, but it's not ours. We don't have the money. We don't have any way to get this building and I don't want to go into debt to get it."

"Yes, we do!" he said.

I thought, what is he talking about?

He motioned for the agent to come over. The realtor handed me a written contract. I looked at it and saw that it was for the purchase of 1002 French Avenue, the address where I was standing. The price was $46,000. The contract was signed by Dr. Al Fornaci and it read, "PAID IN FULL—*IF* ANDREA LIKES IT."

"It now belongs to you. Enjoy your ministry, Andrea," Dr. Al said with a satisfied grin.

A feather could have knocked me over. It was one of those surreal moments. Just months ago, I stood in Pastor Jeff's church as he prayed that God would bring the center a building as a gift. In awe, I stood there speechless and humbled by what God had just done. Dr. Al and Pastor Jeff had never met, yet God used both of them to orchestrate this gift. As my mind was swimming in praise and disbelief, I thought how could Dr. Al just buy a building and then give it away? Was he crazy? In the world's eyes, he probably was. In God's eyes, he was obedient. And Dr. Al's obedience has made a difference in the lives of thousands of children and mothers to this day. For his obedience, I will be forever grateful.

Chapter Ten

Opening Our Doors

On June 1, 1998, the Sanford Crisis Pregnancy Center opened its doors. From the time Dr. Al bought the run-down house, we had exactly eight months to renovate it. Volunteers descended upon the building and brought with them whatever gifts and talents they had to offer. The walls were re-done, the floors leveled and new carpet installed. Windows, sinks, mini-blinds, everything that we needed, including landscaping and painting, was finished in eight months.

The remodeling was a labor of love as men and women from all different denominations came together to work in a spirit of joy and unity. We shared lots of laughs while we worked; the Baptists and the Catholics poked fun at each other and the Methodists and the Lutherans competed to try to out-do each other. In the end, we transformed the old "rat hole" into a warm and inviting cottage just as I had envisioned it on that day when I looked at it through God's eyes.

When our grand opening day arrived, we dedicated our building to God with a special ribbon-cutting ceremony. During the first few weeks after opening, clients slowly found their way to the center. We knew it would take time for the word to get out that we existed. Within a few months, however, we began to see clients daily and the heart of the ministry pumped with compassion as we met each woman with a caring smile and invited her into the counseling room. We prayed daily that every woman who walked through our door would be treated with the dignity and respect she deserved, that her free will would be honored, and that our counselors would be given wisdom by the Holy Spirit as to what to communicate to her.

Heart of the Ministry

Our volunteer lay counselors were (and still are) the heart of the ministry. Wise and mature Christian women were eager to be the hands and eyes of God to the clients He led through our doors. Our volunteers were able to connect easily with our clients since many of them spoke with a voice of experience and were a great source of comfort and wisdom. Behind the doors of the counseling room, God did incredible things. Through ears that were willing to listen and hearts full of compassion, plus a few brochures and fetal models, our trained volunteers ministered to clients.

My mother was one of those volunteers. She stood by my side from the start of the ministry, as she entered her sixth year of sobriety. Mom's heartfelt testimony begged to be shared and the center was the perfect place to share it. Experiencing her own crisis pregnancy with me, she eagerly enrolled in our lay-counseling training course and became equipped to serve. God used her experiences and life lessons to minister to others in the same situation. It amazed me to see clients come in and as I'd offer to help them, they'd ask, "Can I see the lady with the German accent?"

Mom also had the responsibility of managing the boutique at the center. We'd all laugh as donations of used baby clothes came in and had to pass the "Erika eight-point inspection." She would receive it, sniff it, wash it, mend it, iron it, pack it, pray over it and then finally, give it. I'm sure anyone working in ministry would agree that serving becomes a commitment for the whole family. Besides my mom, Dave and my dad have been a big part of the center by faithfully serving as board members and helping to raise support.

As I defined my role of director at the center, I began to see how God was using my 12 years of banking experience to fulfill that responsibility. My job entailed administration, personnel, training, marketing and public awareness. Since the beginning, I have spoken at various churches to raise support for the center, trained new volunteers, and managed the daily operations. I felt like I was born to do that kind of work. Looking back now at those years at the bank, I would have never imagined that I would one day be doing Kingdom work and all that I had learned in banking prepared me for that purpose.

Something in the Water

After two years of working at the center and seeing pregnant women daily, I became pregnant with our third child. While my pregnancy was not a crisis, the reality of carrying a baby added a deeper meaning to the work I was doing. I often felt deep sadness for the babies whose mothers chose to abort them. I can recall once taking a desperate abortion-minded woman into the counseling room when I was 13 weeks pregnant. I did not tell the client that I was pregnant, as I didn't want to be manipulative. She was convinced that ending her pregnancy was her only option and made it clear there was little I could do to console her. She came into the center for one thing—for us to determine how far along she was into her pregnancy. She had already made an appointment for an abortion and the cost of the procedure was dependent on the number of weeks she was pregnant.

As I performed her pregnancy test in our lab and looked for her due date on the pregnancy table chart, I was shocked to learn she was due the same day I was. I wanted so badly to go back into the counseling room and tell her that we were both having our babies on the same day. That our children could possibly be in the same kindergarten class and she might be aborting my baby's best friend. But I knew that would be a form of manipulation and that went against our center's philosophy.

I asked the client if she would like me to educate her on the procedures that the abortion clinics would offer her. She declined. I asked her if she would like me to explain to her the development of her baby and she declined that as well. There was nothing I could say or do. She already made her mind up. Knowing she was leaving the center with intentions of ending her pregnancy made my heart ache. The "savior complex" in me wanted to shake that mother's shoulders and save her baby. I felt helpless and even guilty for being happy about my own pregnancy.

That particular client left the center only to appear in my thoughts during my labor and delivery six months later. At one point, I was given pain medication to take the edge off an intense 18-hour labor that seemed to be going nowhere. I began to think of that client who should have been in the next room delivering her baby along with me. With Dave and my parents by my side, I began to cry and babble things that didn't seem to make any sense.

At first, I was frustrated that they didn't understand me. Between breathless contractions and cries of pain, I cried out, "Why would my baby be allowed to be born and not *her* baby? She should be in the other room next to mine having her baby too!" In Dave's attempt to comfort me, he eventually understood what I was babbling and crying about. As he soothed my aching spirit, I was finally able to let her go and focus on the life to which I was giving birth.

It was 4:50 a.m., on June 7, 2000, when I delivered our beautiful baby girl, Kathryn Anne Krazeise. Weighing in at seven pounds, fourteen ounces, Kate's entry into the world was a family affair, with her daddy, her big brother David, and my parents there to witness her first breath and welcome her. And while this was Kate's birthday, it was a new beginning for my mother, for unlike when David and Daniel were born, my mom was now sober and able to be the kind of grandmother she always wanted to be. Kate's birth was truly a new birth for my mom. It gave her the chance to experience all that she had missed with her other grandchildren.

Mother began making up for lost time within moments of Kate's delivery. I was exhausted from the long labor, so after holding and kissing my baby girl and counting ten toes and ten fingers, the nurse took her away and I fell asleep. All the guys went down to the cafeteria for a victory drink (for all their hard work!) and Mom escorted the nurse and Kate to the nursery and never left my daughter's side for a minute. Mom wanted assurance there was no mix-up with her granddaughter.

A few weeks following Kate's birth, Mom became a lifesaver to me. The delivery caused some complications that required me to undergo minor surgery, which meant complete bed rest and kept me from being self-sufficient for two weeks. Out of that time of brokenness and dependency, God gave me the special gift of having my mother become my caregiver and I loved every minute of having her there to help Kate and me. Whatever suffering and pain I endured was worth every minute as a special bond formed between the three of us.

After a restful three-month maternity leave, I returned to the center part-time. Mom took care of Kate on some of the days I worked. By that time, our son David was entering eighth grade and our son Daniel was starting first grade. During those early years of the center, it was only open four half-days, which allowed me to be home with my children before and after school. Between running the center and caring for our children, my days were full and rewarding. I had a great support system in my husband, my mother and the volunteers at the center. Even Dr. Al fussed over me as if I was one of his kids, worrying that I was doing too much.

Dr. Al Becomes Father Al

Dr. Al loved being a part of the work at the center and visited often. It was his pet project and as an active board member, not only did he raise funds, he also raised awareness. Wherever he went, whenever he spoke, he always talked about the ministry. His presence at the center was a breath of fresh air. His enthusiasm was contagious and his passion unmatched. Every week he brought a potential partner for a tour of the center. On especially difficult days when the volunteers and I felt defeated with heart-breaking cases, his encouragement was just what we needed as he faithfully cheered us on.

A year after the opening of the center, Dr. Al was ordained as a priest and so became Father Al. What an honor and privilege it was to witness his ordination. I could hardly fathom the selfless promise he made to God. During the service, I found myself quietly praying, "Lord, when I grow up, please let me be half the person that Albert J. Fornace has become." The world was a much better place because of him.

At our 3rd Annual Fundraiser Banquet, Father Al and I invited Norma McCorvey to be our keynote speaker. Norma was the infamous "Jane Roe" of the Roe v. Wade decision that legalized abortion in 1973. It was Norma's pregnancy and signature that convinced the U.S. Supreme Court to legalize abortion in our country. Following that landmark decision, Norma ran an abortion clinic in Texas. Approximately thirteen years later, a ten-year-old child relentlessly shared the gospel with Norma and invited her to church. Norma finally gave in to her persistent young friend and attended a Saturday night church service. That night, God reached deep into Norma's heart and lovingly shined His light into the darkest corners of her life and offered her grace, mercy, and forgiveness. Norma accepted His invitation and gave her life to Christ.

Afterward, Norma stepped out of the abortion business and into pro-life ministry as a international spokesperson defending the life of the unborn. She shares her regrets about her role in the Roe v. Wade decision and has dedicated her life to do everything in her power to reverse the ruling that she had previously fought so hard to obtain. She began a ministry called "Roe No More" and in her tender and touching book, *Won by Love,* shares her life story and testimony.

Norma spoke at our banquet and I have to tell you quite honestly that meeting Norma impacted both Father Al and me. She also delighted us in a very special way. We had a fun tradition at our earlier banquets that allowed us to take care of some official business. We needed to pay Father Al for our annual $1.00 lease obligation. I had resisted allowing Father Al to put the building into the name of the center until we reached our five year anniversary, so every year we cheerfully paid him $1.00 to lease it. At each banquet, we would ask if there was anyone who wanted the honor of making our lease payment. That year, Norma McCorvey enthusiastically volunteered! However, instead of paying for one year's lease, she generously paid many years in advance for us. Father Al got the biggest kick out of that and chuckled about it for months.

Passing the Torch

Father Al was only with us for a total of three and a half years before he passed away. He died of congenital heart disease. In his last few months, he was extremely weak and spent his days in a hospital bed. Though his body was failing, his mind was still good and he continued to request updates on the center. I visited my "Apostle Paul" often. During those bedside visits, he encouraged me with words of wisdom and instructions on how to stay in the race and never give up. Even in his weakest moments, he offered me reassurance and strength to stay focused on the mission to which I had been called.

During our three-year friendship, he gave me insight from his own experience that helped prepare me to carry the torch he would soon be passing. While he might have been a prisoner of a failing heart physically, spiritually his heart soared. Even from his hospital bed, he stopped at nothing to finish his race with dignity and the confidence of knowing what awaited him on the other side. While his breath was raspy and his words often unclear, he wanted me to know that he was counting on me to continue the ministry. I struggled with the idea of him not being there beside me. There were many times when I left his bedside distraught and deeply saddened. It was difficult to imagine the ministry without him. He had taught me so much. How could I continue without his help and guidance? Was I ready to do it on my own? Had I learned enough?

Whether I was ready or not, Father Al took his last breath on the first day of June 2001, exactly three years to the day after we opened the doors of the Sanford Crisis Pregnancy Center. Of all the days that Father Al could have left this earth, God chose the anniversary of our grand opening, which gave me peace and assurance knowing God had His hands on Father Al, the ministry and me. Even before God created the world, He knew that our paths would cross in such a way that none of us would ever be the same again. He sent me a 75-year-old priest to serve as my mentor and teacher. He knew that the center would open the first of June and that Father Al would leave us on that same date.

The months to follow were not easy. I missed my beloved friend. If mourning his loss wasn't hard enough, we also faced the uncertainty of the center's future. From a legal standpoint, the building was still in Father Al's name and had become the property of his estate. Attorneys had informed me of the strong possibility that the building might be sold in order to liquidate the estate. If that were to happen, what would we do and where would we go? Unfortunately, I knew I had a hand in that mess.

There had been many occasions when Father Al attempted to transfer the title of the building into the center's name, but I refused. I insisted that we wait until the ministry had five years under its belt, figuring the center would be financially sound and ready to accept the deed by then. In order to protect Father Al's investment, I wanted to establish a solid financial foundation before accepting his generous gift. After his death, we spent a full year with the future of the center up in the air not knowing what was going to happen. We all prayed that somehow it would all work out.

One year following Father Al's death, we received a certified letter in the mail from Father Al's estate. Enclosed was the deed to the building and property. With the deed transferred to our name, the Sanford Crisis Pregnancy Center received ownership of the property debt-free. We became the official owner of the building that our beloved Father Al purchased for us four years earlier.

Over the next few years, we began to serve more and more clients at the center. On one hand, it was sad to see so many women in a crisis situation, but on the other hand, how grateful we were that we could be there to help. As our client load increased, we began to outgrow our little cottage. The thought of building a new center was quickly put to rest and instead, we decided to expand what we already had. We started a building campaign to raise the money needed and in 2006 we expanded the center by adding 1,000 square feet to the existing building.

By doubling our space, we were able to enlarge our boutique, add another office, counseling room and a meeting room to hold board meetings and training classes for new volunteers. Since completing the renovation of the center, we've expanded our services to include an educational program to instruct pregnant women and new moms (new dads, too) on many different topics relating to pregnancy, childcare, and important life skills such as budgeting and nutrition. We've also been able to partner with a mobile sonogram ministry, which has had a tremendous impact on abortion-minded women. I know if Father Al could see the center now and the work we are doing there, he would be so proud.

Divine Appointments

Most of our clients are young women between the ages of 15 and 30, though we have seen some as young as 12 and a few over the age of 40. Many different kinds of women make the long walk from their car to our front door. Over the years, these women have taught us about their diverse cultures, beliefs, pressures, and all too often, about the lack of love in their lives. Their issues, we found, were deeper than the decision to abort or not to abort. Their pregnancies, in most cases, were merely the tip of the iceberg, the by-product of their broken world.

Each of the women who walk through our doors has their own unique story to tell. Of the thousands of women we have seen over the years, most share a common thread. It can be found in each story and seen on each face. It is fear…the kind of fear that immobilizes a person. The mind-numbing fear that makes one consider things they would have never thought of before finding themselves in a crisis pregnancy. To them, abortion seems to be the only option to remedy the crisis. Recognizing this, we see each woman who comes into the center as a divine appointment arranged by God.

"Karla"

One client I remember could have easily been our poster child for someone faced with an unwanted pregnancy. Her name was "Karla." She called the center seeking an abortion. She was the typical girl next door, a 17-year-old senior in high school with plans that didn't include a baby. She had a scholarship to college and told me if her parents found out about her pregnancy, they would be furious. The first thing I told her was that we didn't perform abortions, but we could offer her a free pregnancy test and confidential counseling on her options, so she decided to come in and talk with me.

When she arrived at the center, I could tell she had been crying and reassured her she was in a safe place and everything would be all right. I invited Karla into a counseling room and went over basic information for our intake form. She explained how her pregnancy would devastate her parents, as her father was an elder at a local church. Karla and her boyfriend had been together for a year and a half. Her parents liked him a lot and had recently allowed them to date outside of youth group activities and family events. Becoming sexually involved was not planned, it "just sorta happened one night."

She said that her boyfriend was embarrassed, scared to death and didn't know what to do. They both agreed that an abortion seemed like their only option. I reassured her that since everything we talked about was confidential, I would not call her parents. "I want you to know that I understand this is a scary time for you. I'd like to educate you on your options and I hope you will feel comfortable asking me anything," I explained to her. That seemed to ease her mind and within moments, I sensed a genuine connection of trust.

A pregnancy test confirmed that Karla was in fact pregnant and approximately ten weeks along. Her first question was, "How is an abortion done?" I explained to her the medical procedure, including the risks and consequences she should consider. I showed her a plastic model of a uterus as a visual aid to help her see the anatomy of her reproductive organs and what would take place. As she listened, I could tell she was grasping the severity of the procedure. One of the models had a ten-week fetus inside the uterus. As she looked at it carefully, she said, "This baby is very developed. What is it, 20 weeks or so?"

"No, Karla," I told her truthfully, "that baby is ten weeks old."

Her eyes filled with tears as she realized the baby she was carrying was at such a developed stage. I explained that her baby has had a heartbeat since 18 days and brain activity since 42 days. She was completely surprised and continued to examine the model she held in her hands. "What am I going to do?" she cried. "My parents are going to be so disappointed in me, but I can't end this baby's life because of what I did."

I wrapped my arms around her and told her, "God will give you the strength to do the right thing, starting first with telling your parents. We all make mistakes, but we can make new choices every day." I was not about to wave a finger of judgment, she already felt enough guilt and shame to last a lifetime. I did my best to convey my love and support. Sadly, over the years I've heard many "religious" girls say they would rather have an abortion than face the condemnation of their church. What a sad state of the body of Christ, if we are in fact the fuel that drives a girl to an abortion clinic to end the life of her child.

Our session lasted for an hour. Before she left, we set up an action plan. First, she would go to her boyfriend and bring him up-to-date on what she had learned at the center. Then she had to go to her parents with a humble spirit and tell them. I warned her, "Be prepared that they will be upset. Give them time to process it all. Tell them you came here to seek counseling. That will show them you are attempting to right the wrong. And after the shock of it passes, they'll help you through this." She was broken and afraid, and yet at the same time, eager to unload the heavy burden she was carrying. As she cried, I took her hands and prayed that God would give her the words to speak, that He would prepare her parents' hearts to receive the news, and that their love for her would guide them through it all.

As she was leaving, she gave me a hug and thanked me repeatedly. I told her to call me in a few days to tell me how things went and let me know if there was anything I could do to help. My heart was heavy for her while I watched her leave and get into her car. She was so young and overwhelmed. I wanted so much to rescue her and protect her. As she drove away, I lifted her up to God and reminded myself that He loved Karla more than I could imagine and that He would take it from there.

I learned early on that there came a certain point in counseling where you stop and God takes over. My job was simply to plant the seed. He does the watering. Though we seldom get to see the fruit of our labor, in this case, God allowed me to see His handiwork. About a week later, Karla called me. She sounded different, much more confident and at peace. She had told her parents the following day. They were upset, of course, but they didn't stop loving her. Within a few days, they had decided to keep the baby. She was due five weeks after graduation. Her mother and grandmother rallied around her, offering to help her with the baby so that she could attend community college. Her dreams, though slightly different, were still intact.

Over the next few months, Karla and her boyfriend came in several times to watch videos preparing them for childbirth, prenatal care and caring for a newborn. One week before her due date, Karla gave birth to a healthy six-pound, four-ounce baby boy. Praise God!

"Toni"

The Sanford CPC had only been open for a few months when "Toni" came in. She was a memorable client whose crisis was out of the ordinary, at least for us. Toni was a member of Father Al's parish and he had advised her to come see us. She was 35 years old and had just found out that she was pregnant with quadruplets when she came to us emotionally distraught.

Prior to that morning, Toni thought she was carrying twins. She was 16 weeks along and it was only hours earlier that her doctors discovered she was carrying four fetuses and they strongly suggested that she "selectively reduce" her pregnancy. They explained to her that in multiple births, it was rare for all the babies to survive if left in the womb. They wanted her to eliminate two of the fetuses to give the remaining two a greater chance of survival. The doctors told Toni that if she did not reduce the babies from four to two, she might lose them all.

Toni did not want to make such a painful decision. Which two babies would she and her husband sacrifice for the sake of the other two? I struggled with my own composure as I watched her vacillate between the hope of watching her four children grow up and then gut wrenching sobs, as she could not bear that heavy decision. Nothing had prepared me for a situation like that. All I knew to do was to pray. The other counselors and I prayed for wisdom on how to counsel Toni. On one hand, we clearly knew that God had created each child, but at the same time, medical statistics offered a real possibility of losing them all.

As she cried in despair, we all gathered around her and prayed for God's strength and wisdom. We knew Toni was the only one who could make that decision. It was between her and God. While I had never been in a position like hers, I tried to be logical, rational and compassionate. Ultimately, all I could do was anchor my faith in the fact that God would not let her down.

After we finished praying, there was silence. Then Toni wiped the tears from her eyes and looked up. She said in a quiet, yet bold voice, "I'm not taking one of these babies' lives. I will carry them all. If God wants to take them, then He can, but I won't." Toni made the decision to completely trust Him and put her four babies in His hands.

Throughout her pregnancy, Toni visited us often. Her doctors were not happy with her decision and made it perfectly clear that they were not responsible for the outcome. We prayed daily for Toni and the babies. She remained healthy and happy, although she was miserably uncomfortable and could barely walk at times. I have to be very honest here— Toni's belly was the biggest I'd ever seen and even her stretch marks had stretch marks. I hurt just looking at her!

By the time she was 20 weeks, she learned that all four babies were girls. At 25 weeks, Toni was confined to round-the-clock bed rest. We knew that she would not carry them to full term, so each week that passed was a huge victory for the babies.

Our center, along with her church, gave her the biggest baby shower anyone could imagine. Toni received four of everything—four cribs, four highchairs, double strollers and four matching outfits in every color and style. The biggest challenge was finding four car seats to fit in her small car.

We contacted a local car dealership and they donated a brand new minivan that had four custom car seats made especially for the girls. Toni soon became a local celebrity and people in the community helped out in many ways.

On November 3, 1998, Toni gave birth to four healthy preemie girls, each one weighing less than two pounds. What a miracle it was! As each little girl entered the world, it was obvious that there was a fighter's spirit inside her tiny little body.

Toni's husband invited a few of us from the center to visit Toni that day. I put on scrubs and went into the neonatal unit to see the babies. They were so tiny they could fit in their father's hand. I was reminded how small we are in comparison to our heavenly Father and how He holds each of us in the palm of His hand. What an honor it was to be a part of something so incredible.

As I looked at each baby and studied her features and the sounds of her cry, I tried to imagine which two Toni would have picked to eliminate. Thank God, Toni never made that decision, but simply trusted. What an awesome lesson that was for me as I ventured into that new ministry. God was teaching me to walk with Him—not ahead or behind—and that He Himself would be the shelter and refuge for many women yet to come.

"Shannon"

Over the years of ministry, we have seen the heartache of countless women who have suffered the emotional consequences of having an abortion. Post-abortion syndrome is very real and emotionally crippling for many women. "Shannon" was one of them. Within a year following her abortion, Shannon began experiencing signs of post-abortion trauma. She was having terrible nightmares and flashbacks of the day she ended her pregnancy. The guilt, shame and regret were tearing her apart. Shannon already had another child who was four years old and she found herself disconnecting from that child. Despite being raised in the church, Shannon felt God could never forgive her or love her after what she had done. Not only that, but she felt she could never forgive herself.

Post-abortion trauma affects millions of women and even men. For some, there is what's known as the "sleeper affect," where the impact of their abortion doesn't reveal itself until many years afterward. We wanted Shannon to know that the despair and shame she felt could be lifted and her life did not have to be defined by the choice she once made. We assured her she was not alone and that God could bring her back to wholeness and help her accept the forgiveness and grace He offers. Laurie Wren was leading a group Bible study called "Forgiven and Set Free" and we asked Shannon to consider enrolling. It was a specially designed eight-week study to help restore and heal a woman's heart following an abortion. Shannon was reluctant at first, but later changed her mind and enrolled.

For eight weeks, I watched Shannon come into the center for the session. In the beginning, she would walk in with her head down, embarrassed to be there. As the sessions progressed, her spirit became lighter and I could tell she was beginning to see her way through what must have seemed like a dark forest with no way out.

During her journey to healing, Shannon accepted responsibility for her abortion decision and eventually came to a place of peace where she would honor her baby's life. She learned of God's great love and forgiveness—and how Jesus gave His life on the cross for all her transgressions, including her abortion decision. Each week she experienced the power of healing and wholeness that comes with godly sorrow and repentance and in the end she was able to forgive herself.

God promises in Micah 7:19 that "our iniquities are hurled into the depths of the sea."

At the final session of her Bible study, I witnessed her leaving the center giving Laurie hugs and heartfelt thanks for being there during those difficult weeks. I'll never forget what I saw that day, as Shannon experienced closure on the emotional pain she had carried for so long. As she hugged Laurie at the door, she was a completely different woman than I saw just eight weeks earlier. There was a radiant glow on her face and a joy that emanated from her heart that only comes from experiencing God's grace in such a powerful way. As she walked out the door, she paused and turned back around to us. Her eyes filled with tears and a smile came over her beautiful face. She looked at Laurie and me, lifted her hands skyward, and cried out, "I'm free!" Indeed she was. Forgiven and set free, Shannon was living proof that Jesus' death was not in vain.

I could fill volumes recording the countless client testimonies and miracles seen at the center. The ones I've mentioned here represent hundreds of women that I have been honored to serve over the years, each one teaching me the power of God's grace and sovereignty. Witnessing their anguish and desperation has filled my heart with compassion and empathy for what my own mom must have experienced when she learned she was pregnant with me.

I am forever grateful for those two Ukrainian women who reached out to my mother and unknowingly saved me. Had abortion been legal then, I would not be here giving this testimony. Those women put love into action by caring for a teenage unwed mother and seeing her through her pregnancy. While there weren't any crisis pregnancy centers in those days for my mother to go, those women did the work of a CPC. The ministry of crisis pregnancy centers boils down to one woman reaching out to another woman.

Laurie Is Called

Shannon was one of the first clients that Laurie led to post-abortion healing. Within three years of serving as the center's client services director, God called Laurie to full-time post-abortion counseling. Laurie put her passion into practice as the Founder and Director of Reveille Ministry, Inc. where she now leads many more post-abortive women to healing and recovery.

Not only does Laurie counsel clients, she also trains and equips lay people in the community to lead abortion recovery groups in area churches. Through Laurie's faithfulness and obedience, she has helped countless women who have suffered silently for years find healing and restoration following an abortion experience.

Within a year of Laurie's ministry launch, Shannon became a trained volunteer, leading other post-abortive women to recovery as well. Since the day Laurie and I met, we have remained close friends and we continue to partner in each other's ministries.

Chapter Eleven

You Can't Put Ministry in a Box

O ne of the biggest lessons I've learned in ministry is that you can't put ministry in a nice neat package. While I had one idea of whom I was serving — the abortion-minded woman, God on the other hand began to put other people in my path He wanted me to also notice. God expanded my vision beyond the walls of the pregnancy center to see my corner of the world through His eyes. Our center was situated on the main drag of town, which I knew was a great location to reach hurting women, but what I didn't expect was the hurting to include homeless, prostitutes, crack addicts, drug dealers, and children caught in the crossfire of poverty and despair. It was a mission field I never envisioned. On any given day, I could look out the windows of the center and see drug dealers and prostitutes pass by right before my eyes.

Because of the constant "activity" that took place within one block of our building, we pretty much stayed out of our neighbors' way. We didn't mess with them and they didn't mess with us. They all came to recognize me as I drove to our mailbox down the street each day. As I made my circle around the block, some would nod or wave at me and I'd do the same. There was a kind of unstated mutual respect between us. On rare occasions, I would try to make small talk if someone was walking along our property when I was taking out the trash, but most of the time they avoided me and pretended I wasn't there.

Two doors down from the center was a business for day laborers. On occasion, the manager would stop in the center to visit and educate me on "the ways of the streets." He would tell me about the prostitutes in the neighborhood and how they were all hooked on crack cocaine. According to him, they lived simply for their next hit. If they could turn two or three tricks a day, that would provide enough money for them to buy some food, beer, and crack. If they were lucky, they could also get a much-needed shower. I often wondered about those women, imagining what had happened in their lives to bring them to that place. I mean, each of these women where once little girls that played with paper dolls who never dreamed of aspiring to this profession.

Those young women hung around the labor pool, but they weren't interested in picking oranges for the day. Their business brought them to the labor pool doors just as the men were returning from working in the groves. The manager was constantly running them off; however, they would usually just go around to the side of the building and coax the men from there. About a dozen of the girls lived in the woods or vacant houses just two blocks away.

The manager told me some of their names and warned me which ones to avoid, as they would have no problem tearing my hair out if I got in their way. One day he gave me a mini-lecture saying, "Andrea, all they want is money and it doesn't matter whom they get it from or how they get it. It's called survival. Your money is as good as the orange pickers'! They'll steal you blind if you drop your guard." I considered myself warned.

An Unlikely Teacher

There was one prostitute who I saw often walking in the neighborhood. On occasion I would watch her from my window and wonder what her life was like. If I saw her outside, I tried not to make eye contact. But one particular day, as I was putting trash in the dumpster, I turned around and to my surprise she was only about 10 feet away. Her head was down as she walked along. Then she looked up and I think she was equally as startled as I was. It was a little awkward, but I asked nervously, "How ya doing?"

I figured she'd just walk past me and not say a word. But surprisingly she approached me. She caught me off guard when she extended her hand and introduced herself, "Hi, my name is Lisa." I liked her immediately. She had a shy smile and a warm demeanor. Her frame was petite and she looked as though she was once very athletic. With her hair over-grown and covering her face, it was hard to make out her eyes. Her next question surprised me even more than her introduction. "Would you mind if I took some things out of your dumpster? I mean, since you're throwing them away anyway. There's usually some stuff I can use."

It seemed almost every week I threw away donated items that really weren't suitable for our clients. We were always grateful for the bags of used baby clothes that people gave us as long as they were in good condition, but some were beyond salvaging. Those were the things that Lisa wanted and was grateful to have. She said she knew many folks in the neighborhood who were happy to receive the stained and buttonless items. I was impressed with her generous spirit and was quick to tell her to salvage whatever she could.

Within minutes, we were like two old friends having a heart-to-heart conversation. The only difference was that we were having it over a dumpster. I tenderly asked her what her struggles were and why she was on the streets. The thin

38-year-old woman freely shared the burdens of her heart, explaining she had been "out here for two years and wouldn't wish this on anybody." Her father died about ten months ago and her boyfriend had been killed in a motorcycle accident two years earlier. Tears spilled from her eyes when she told me how the two important men in her life were gone. As for the cocaine, as it often happens, what started out as recreational drug use years ago turned into a habit and later became an addiction. Out of desperation, she ended up on the streets trying to survive.

My heart broke for her as she spoke fondly of the father she missed. Just listening to her somehow seemed to validate her pain. While I stood there, an occasional thought flashed through my mind of the things the labor pool manager told me. Was I being too naïve? Was this a ploy to hustle some money from me? Was she sizing me up, with plans to turn on me and beat me up?

Lisa asked nothing of me except the discarded baby clothes. She eased any discomfort I felt when she mentioned that she and the other women had talked about me. That made me a little nervous at first, wondering what could these women have against me. "Andrea, we all agree that what you're doing at the center is a good thing. Don't be afraid of us. We look out for you in this neighborhood. No one's gonna mess with you," she explained. My heart skipped a beat. Had she read my mind? As it turned out, they were more afraid of me, fearing I'd make trouble for them. It was a rough neighborhood and I didn't want to make enemies with anyone. What a relief to know, if anything, they were watching *my* back. Imagine that!

Our conversation lasted about 20 minutes. I assured her that I would be praying for her great loss and for her safety. I also told her that I would be here if she ever wanted to talk, "just woman to woman." She smiled and said, "Thanks! I'll see ya sometime." I really didn't expect to talk to her again, but thought what a sweet encounter we'd just had. I felt so blessed to have met her and privileged that she would be so transparent with me. She was honest and candid about who she was and what she did. I felt honored that she trusted me with something dear to her heart—the personal hurts of her life.

To my surprise, Lisa came into the center the next week. I was so happy to see her. She gave me a great big hug. Her damp hair smelled of Irish Spring soap. When I commented on how fresh she smelled, she said that one of the neighbors let her use their water hose to clean up. With her wet wavy blonde hair combed back, I could see her green eyes and the weathered lines around them. Dressed in black faded jeans and a white tank top, I invited her into our kitchen area for some coffee.

While we talked, she told me about her children. Lisa had a 17-year-old son and two young daughters, but lost custody of them due to her drug addiction. She bragged about her son having a baby boy of his own and how much the baby looked like his granddaddy, the father she lost. We talked about her family, where she attended school and things she'd like to do one day. The idea of having her own place and a flower garden made her smile. The more I became acquainted with Lisa, the more I liked her. I was impressed with her sweet spirit and how life on the streets had not hardened her heart.

For the next few months, Lisa came into the center occasionally to visit, usually with a handful of beautiful flowers that she had picked from a nearby garden. She knew her flowers well, naming each type and their blooming season. By that time, I was aware of her living conditions and I would offer her toiletry items, clothes, and a blanket here and there. She was very unassuming and I found it easy to give to her because she never asked for anything. The problem was what I gave her often was stolen by the other girls.

We talked about her drug addiction and what it would take for her to overcome it. What I didn't understand, but came to learn later, was how intense the addiction to crack cocaine was and how bad she hated what she did. It reminded me of the Apostle Paul when he spoke of the things he hated and yet still did. Since I had never used drugs, it was hard to understand why she couldn't just quit. While I witnessed what alcohol did to my parents, her addiction was much more intense and all consuming. The desire was so strong for Lisa, that her only purpose for living was the pursuit of drugs and the experience of a high that lasted just a few minutes. And if that meant performing immoral acts to support her habit, then it's what she would do. It was all a mystery to me, but I listened and learned from her.

Lisa taught me a great deal about the powerful compulsion drugs can hold over someone. With her eyes glassy and speech slurred, I could soon tell when Lisa had just had a hit of crack. I told her that I didn't want her to come around the center high and she respected that. So when we did see her she was sometimes antsy and nervously craving her next hit. There were times I just wanted to hold her hostage and not let her leave, knowing what she felt compelled to do. But I understood this battle was one she had to fight on her own and more importantly, a battle she had to *want* to fight. I was glad that she always allowed me to pray for her and as her tears flowed, I knew in those briefs moments Lisa's heart belonged to God and not to the streets.

Lisa's honesty about her life and addiction opened my eyes to another world. Through her eyes, I saw the harsh reality of drugs and sex, which helped me understand how women like her exist. She shared with me the drama of some of the other women and told me stories of greed, theft, revenge, violence, and the emotional and spiritual hurts that made life unbearable at times. Lisa, being one of the oldest, considered herself the "mother" of the younger girls on the street. It made her sad to see girls only 18 or 19 years old fall prey to a lifestyle that could eventually kill them.

Over coffee one morning, she told me something I will never forget. She explained that at times, when she'd had a good paying customer, she would buy enough drugs to share with one of the younger girls. I couldn't believe what I was hearing. Why would this mother figure share her drugs with a teenager? But in a twisted way, Lisa was looking out for her, and she said to me, "I look at this way, Andrea—me sharing my drugs with her means a day this little gal doesn't have to have sex with a stranger." There was no pleasure in performing sex acts for money. Simply put, it was a means to an end. While I didn't agree with her choices, I began to understand her world and the things she did to survive.

Occasionally, when she visited me at the center, Lisa would call her mother to find out how her children were doing. She would tell me about them and because we both had daughters, Lisa was interested in hearing about my Kate, too. Sometimes when she talked about her daughters, her laughter would turn to tears, recognizing the mess she had made of her life. I always hoped that hearing about her kids would motivate Lisa to get into drug rehab and fight for them. I knew Lisa and I lived in two different worlds, but we shared the common bond of motherhood that couldn't be discounted. Truth is, when you strip away the outer layers of Lisa's life, she was like any other woman, longing to love and be loved with dreams of a better life for her children.

As a young girl, Lisa believed in God, attended church often and knew the Bible fairly well. However, she felt a deep sense of shame. "How could God love me after all I've done?" she would ask me. I often reminded her of God's love and that there was nothing she could do to stop Him from loving her. She said she talked to Him often when she was afraid, especially at night while sleeping in the woods or under someone's porch. She asked God to protect her when the "johns" would come around and harass some of the girls. Because most of Lisa's clients were "regulars," she didn't have to enlist a pimp for protection. Regardless, it was a violent way of life and someone was always getting beat up, usually for stealing someone's customer. Each time Lisa left the center, I prayed that God would somehow intervene in her life. I wondered what it was going to take to get Lisa out of the stronghold in which Satan had her.

Then she came to me one day and said that she had a court appearance in a couple of days. It was only for a loitering charge but her public defender had prepared her for the reality of sitting in jail for 18 days for the violation. I immediately thought it was the break she needed. She would go to jail for almost three weeks and get clean. Her mom always told her that she was welcome back home if she was clean. Lisa and I talked about how her bleak situation could be her big break. It was strange to think of jail as a route to freedom, but the more we talked, the more determined she was to make this work.

Lisa knew her family was supportive and loved her. Two days prior to her court appearance, I drove her to her mother's home where they had a sweet reunion. They had not seen each other in nine months and Lisa had been drug-free now for three days. I saw walking, living, breathing hope. Lisa was ready for a new start and we were all hopeful. I visited her twice while she stayed with her mother and took her out to lunch one day so we could talk and pray. After lunch, I treated her to a new haircut that would make a good impression on the judge.

Like a puppy that just had a bath, Lisa was clean and fresh. Several long hot showers and the comfort of her mother's home made life on the streets seem like a thing of the past. At her mother's request, I took several pictures of them together arm in arm with my digital camera. Lisa told her mother and me she decided to go into rehab after her short stint in jail. She wanted the judge to know that she was serious and ready to fight for her kids. I contacted a personal attorney friend of mine who agreed to legally represent Lisa free of charge.

The days passed quickly and she was emotionally ready to go. Lisa asked if I had a spare Bible for her to take to jail. Not only did I give her a Bible, but also I gave her a journal and pens so she could study while she was there. It was a bittersweet morning seeing her go to court and leave with the officers.

While Lisa served her time, I arranged for her to have a bed at the local drug rehab upon her release. During her time in jail, I had no contact with her. The day before her release, her mother asked me if I could pick Lisa up from the jail and bring her home for a night before going into rehab.

The day of her release, I waited outside the gate of the correctional facility. I was eager to see her. As she came around the corner carrying her Bible and a pile of papers, she was so excited and happy to see me. I braced myself as I saw her running toward me to give me an embrace that only someone experiencing freedom could. As she hugged me, she said, "I have so much to tell you!" She explained that she had done "lots and lots of journaling" as she spent time alone with God. As she got in the car, I noticed a bandage on her left hand. In her excitement, she forgot all about an infection caused by a spider biting her in jail. As she unwrapped the bandage she said, "I need to see a doctor, but first I want some real food!"

Before heading to breakfast, we stopped at a convenience store near the correctional facility. Lisa ran in to buy a pack of cigarettes, a Snickers candy bar and a Mountain Dew. She came back to the car and asked if I minded if she smoked a cigarette before we went to breakfast. I stayed in the car where it was cool and watched her from a distance. Lisa walked over to two guys who were standing outside the store and easily struck up a conversation as one offered to light her cigarette. I could see how much she was enjoying her freedom as she would take a long drag of her cigarette and then stretch her arms out to embrace the sunshine.

As I watched her from behind the tinted windows of my car, something happened that captivated me. Coming from behind where Lisa was standing, a pretty monarch butterfly fluttered past her. As it flew around, it caught Lisa's attention. She stopped talking to the men and watched the butterfly flit around her and eventually into the woods about 20 feet away. In a span of 40 seconds or so, her eyes never left the butterfly until it was out of sight. She watched in wonder with a sweet smile on her face.

Once the butterfly was out of sight, she resumed her conversation and took one more long drag. She then smashed the half-smoked cigarette on the concrete and ran to the car. As we drove off, she told me about the conversation she had with the two guys and how they had just gotten out of jail, too, and what their plans were. Then to my surprise she said, "Oh, Andrea! There was this beautiful butterfly that I was watching. It was so big and the colors were so brilliant! It was so cool!"

Lisa's enthusiasm was refreshing. Little did she know I was watching her watch the butterfly. Like that butterfly, Lisa was just as beautiful and had been given a new chance to spread her wings and fly. We headed to a local Denny's for a Grand Slam breakfast fit for a hungry queen and talked for two hours. After breakfast, I took her home to spend the night with her mother, with plans to enter rehab the following day.

The next morning, I got a call from Lisa's mother saying that Lisa needed to go the emergency room because her hand was badly infected. I drove to their house, picked her up, and headed to the hospital. Knowing she might have to wait several hours, she brought her Bible and we stopped to get her some lunch. Because I had to be home to see Kate off the school bus, I had to leave Lisa to wait alone at the ER. I left around 1:00 p.m. and gave her enough money for a cab to get back home. We planned to talk on the phone later that evening to see how things went and make arrangements for the next day.

Hours went by and I didn't hear from Lisa. By 9:00 p.m. her mother called and said Lisa wasn't home yet. I called the emergency room and a nurse informed me that a doctor had seen Lisa and released her around 4:00 p.m. The following day, still no one had seen or heard from her. We were all feeling pretty anxious. Her mother finally shared her suspicions with me. Her hunch was that "she had gone back to the streets." I was devastated. I couldn't accept that. Lisa had come this far and was so close. How could this happen? Why would she do this?

Two weeks went by and I heard nothing from Lisa. Each day that passed without any word from her brought me closer to the realization of the stronghold drugs had on Lisa. Finally, one day I asked another one of the local prostitutes who was walking by the center if she had seen Lisa. The young woman told me that Lisa was back in the neighborhood but was too ashamed to come see me. I didn't know what to say or think. I asked God, "What do you want me to do for Lisa? Am I supposed to just wash my hands of her and let her go?"

The following day, I saw the same woman walk by and I asked her if she would deliver a letter to Lisa for me. The note explained that I loved Lisa and that I was still there for her. I knew deep in my heart that God was speaking through me and His message was clear. He wanted Lisa to know that He still loved her and His love wasn't conditional. His love for her was about grace, the kind of love none of us deserves. My role was simply to be His messenger—to tell Lisa there was nothing she could do to stop God from loving her. Three days later, Lisa came into the center to see me. I hugged her as she cried in my arms with disappointment and shame.

From then on, it was back to where we began. Lisa was back on the streets and would come and visit me on occasion. This time, however, there was a difference. Lisa's mom would call me regularly to see how she was doing. I had become the liaison between them. With Lisa living on the streets, her mother never had any idea of where or how she was. She always hoped for the best and wanted to know that Lisa was okay. For the most part, I spared her mother the details of Lisa's life. I assured her that Lisa was eating and looked good. Her mom would convey messages from her kids. I gladly became the bridge between the two of them, giving her mother some measure of peace. I remained hopeful that one day there would be another reunion for them and another chance for Lisa.

Early one February morning, my day began like any other. I got my kids off to school, checked phone messages, and then headed off to the center. My cell phone rang and on the line was a police investigator. He informed me that Lisa had been murdered in the early morning hours and her body was found on the railroad tracks just a half-mile from the center. The investigator found my phone number in Lisa's wallet.

My knees felt wobbly. My thoughts raced. This had to be a sick joke. He couldn't mean *my* Lisa. Surely they must have the wrong woman and *my* Lisa would walk into the center later that day and we would have a good laugh about it all. But Lisa never came. The hours and days that followed were a blur. Time had no real substance except to remind me that we are finite creatures and our lives are fragile.

The local newspaper shot out a sensational story of the murder. The article showed the street side of Lisa—not the human side I knew. There were no kind words, nothing humane, just facts and a horrible mug shot of her. The Lisa

I knew had feelings, dreams, hopes, and regrets. She was a human being that deserved better than that. The tabloid write-up failed miserably in describing who she really was.

I contacted the newspaper and boldly asked them to write another story about Lisa. "Make it a human interest piece," I pleaded. She deserved better than the cold, unfeeling words that outlined her life in the paper. They agreed and wrote another story showing the Lisa I had seen underneath the earthy exterior—the once-happy, church-going daughter, the straight-A student, the award-winning track star with the heart of a mother who died by the hands of a crazed killer.

With the help of a few others, I put together a memorial service for Lisa. We held it at the Central Florida Dream Center in Sanford. Lisa's family and friends from her former days gathered together to share stories and remember Lisa. With her mother's help, we made a memorial table displaying childhood photos of Lisa, flowers, candles and some of Lisa's favorite things. Many of us spoke from our hearts and told of our joy in knowing Lisa. I shared how this 38-year-old woman had changed me and how she had become one of the most unlikely and best teachers in my life.

Almost two years following Lisa's death, justice was served. Authorities charged a local man for her rape and murder. They were able to link her death with another prostitute's death three years earlier. The defendant who was charged had been arrested for raping six women, two of whom he murdered. The rapist was very selective choosing these women because he believed they wouldn't make good witnesses. They were drug addicts, prostitutes, and homeless women. Time after time, authorities connected this man to the victims—his DNA was found on five of the six women—but most of the cases fell apart because the victims disappeared, were mentally unstable, or refused to cooperate.

In Lisa's homicide, the defendant's DNA was present as well as the detection of his monitoring ankle device placing him where Lisa's body was found. The killer was pronounced guilty and sentenced to life in prison.

Beautiful Souls

After Lisa's death, I felt my definition of being a Christian expand. Today, I can't look at a prostitute or homeless woman without feeling compassion, knowing that underneath the outer layers of dysfunction and addictions, there is a beautiful soul underneath. While Lisa was an admitted addict, in the core of her heart, she knew Christ. So what was the definition of a Christian? Was it broad enough to encompass the prostitutes, drug users, homeless and other broken people of the world?

One thing I know, Lisa equipped me to be a better friend and better counselor because of her honesty and transparency about the things with which she struggled. That's why, at times, it was refreshing to share a burger or have a conversation with her over a dumpster. At times, she displayed the qualities of Jesus in ways that I wouldn't have seen if I had only looked at the outside layers of her life. I could have easily missed the point of the gospel if I had responded to Lisa based on her outward appearance. And while I'm not responsible for the choices she made, I am responsible for pointing her and others toward the hope we have in Jesus.

In the Gospels, Christ cared about simple human dignities. He talked to and touched the lepers. He ate meals with outcasts and wept with those who wept. Since knowing Lisa, my husband, my daughter Kate (now 7 years old) and I befriended some homeless guys at a local soup kitchen. Over the course of a few months, we became acquainted with them; two in particular, Mike and James.

They told us of a wooded area they called their home. Dave and I (and another couple from church) asked them if we could visit them sometime at their campsite, bring some sandwiches and sit by the fire and talk. They eagerly said yes. Mike asked, "Will Miss Kate be coming, too?" They were always kind and polite to our daughter, as she often came to the soup kitchen to serve with us. I told them I would bring Kate if they agreed to behave and not use foul language or drink alcohol in her presence. They readily agreed.

On Christmas day, the five of us (our friends, Dave, Kate, and I) went to visit Mike and James at their campsite in the woods. As we all sat around the fire eating and laughing, we had a great time talking about their days in the military and the towns they grew up in. Watching the glow of the fire coals, it felt like we were camping out with old friends instead of visiting a homeless camp.

When it was time for us to leave, we asked if there was anything in particular they needed. We figured they might request a new tent, some socks, blankets, or a cooler, anything to make their lives a little more comfortable. Instead they said, "You just gave us everything we needed." We were puzzled and then they explained, "By just hanging out with us around our fire and talking, you made us feel human. That's all we need." Those words pierced our hearts. The simple dignity of feeling human is all they wanted. Loving God's people isn't that hard. No matter what the outer man looks like, we all long to feel we have worth.

"Dear children, let us not love with words or tongue but with *actions* and in truth." (1 John 3:18, emphasis mine.) God makes divine appointments for each one of us all the time. Has God placed someone in your life that He is calling you to notice, to reach out to, to share His love with? Treating people with dignity, it's not that hard. And let me assure you, we are all more equipped than we think we are.

Chapter Twelve

Truth That Waited a Lifetime

Working in ministry can certainly exhaust one's emotions. It's next to impossible to really love people without putting your heart on the line. That's why I've always believed that taking time away for rest and relaxation is necessary for a healthy heart and mind. When I get the chance to go on vacation, I return refreshed and recharged with new enthusiasm and energy. During the summer of 2005, my family and I spent our vacation at Longboat Key, Florida. That particular year marked our seventh year of ministry at the center and our fifth vacation at Longboat Key.

Like other vacations we'd taken in recent years, my whole family went together, including Dave and me, David, Daniel, Kate, and my mom and dad. All of us agreed that beach vacations were what we liked best. After we found a little piece of paradise on the tranquil Gulf Coast, we've returned time and time again to soak up every treasured minute on God's glorious playground.

What we liked best about this spot was the peacefulness and the warm gentle breezes the Gulf of Mexico offered. The sound of water and sea gulls always helped me clear my head so I could reconnect with God and the people I loved most. One of our favorite activities was to walk along the crystal clear shores looking for new finds that the tide brought in. Sometimes Dave and the kids would go off in one direction while Mom and I would go in the other. Dad would usually hang out at the base (where the lounge chairs and umbrella were staked in the sand) and do some snorkeling. The treasure hunters among us were always anxious to return to the base and show off our prize finds. The one who collected the greatest find was declared the "great white hunter."

The long lazy days in the sun and slow walks on the beach made for great conversations and diligent soul-searching. I don't know if I can explain it, but there is something incredible about standing on the shore facing the ocean. For me, I realize just how small I am compared to God. It gives me a deep desire to clear my conscience and be in perfect fellowship with Him. I am always in awe of the waves, the tide coming in and going out, and the glorious sunsets painted across the evening sky.

I love losing myself in the wonder of His creation, to think of how the earth spins itself effortlessly on its journey around the sun to make a single day. And without fail, every day there is a sunrise and a sunset. I watch the tide come in to where I am standing and wonder, who told the tide it could only come to this point? Why doesn't it come in any closer? Who told the sun to shine on the gulf shore in all its brilliance?

God, of course. He knows exactly how many grains of sand are on Longboat's shore. Every part of His creation stands at attention waiting to display His glory, waiting to show off the hands that created them. He is the tide's keeper. He is the sun's keeper. He is also the keeper of my life, my soul, my heart—and yours as well. He knows what's best for us and He cares for us more than we ever could.

He reveals His truth, His purpose and His will for us in His perfect timing. Like the course of a day when our planet aligns itself to make a single day, I know He has aligned events of my life to get me to the place I am now. I know He aligned the events of my life to get me to the point where I was the summer of 2005. I see now there was nothing random about my being on Longboat Key that summer just as there is nothing random about His universe. It's the timing of grace—when a series of events come together to fulfill His purpose.

One morning, Mom and I headed off down the beach to begin our treasure hunt. I could hear the gentle lapping of waves washing up on the shore. A few seagulls stood as sentries nearby in the white sand. As I stared at the ocean, I was reminded of one of God's promises found in Micah 7:19 that says my "sins are hurled into the depths of the seas." Walking along staring at the bigness of the ocean, I had a heightened sense of God's presence and I knew there was a certain matter that I longed to address with Mom. There was one issue I had harbored for as long as I could remember and for some reason that morning seemed to be the God-ordained time to resolve it. I had not planned it, but standing in the vastness of God's creation, I felt He was prompting me to ask the question that had waited for years of healing to first take place. I felt it was now safe to ask my mom about Giulio, my biological father.

Truth Revealed

All these years and I knew so little about him. I had no idea what he looked like or anything about his relationship with my mother. The only thing she ever said was, "He was a bad man and hurt me deeply." Early in my life, she led me to believe that Giulio had no interest in us and abandoned us when he learned of Mom's pregnancy. She did tell a story about him once, when I was a teenager. She told me that when I was nine months old and we lived in Germany, Giulio tried to kidnap me. She said that Giulio crawled up the fire escape of Oma's second floor apartment and tried to come into my bedroom through the window, while I was asleep in my crib. Mom walked into the room to check on me and caught him looking in the window. She screamed and he fled. I always thought that was kind of odd. He wanted to kidnap me? What was he going to do once he kidnapped me—sell me to the Mafia or something?

So the only information I amassed over the years about my father was that he was a heartless man, he deeply hurt my mother, he rejected both of us, he had no interest in us and did nothing to support us. For my entire life, I thought of him as the man who didn't want me. To be quite honest, I never lost any sleep over it and that was probably because I had a dad in Don who loved me. And truthfully, can you miss something you've never had?

Over the years, people asked me if I ever thought of searching for my real father. I already had a dad who adopted and raised me, so searching for a stranger whom I never knew somehow felt like it would betray Don. What was the point of searching for someone I believed didn't want me? What would I gain? To hear him say, "Yeah, I didn't want you. Now what do you want to make of that?" But, over the last few years, I had begun to wonder if there wasn't more to the story.

For Mom and me, these last few years had been good for us. There was closure to the past alcohol abuse, the neglect, and her anger toward me. She was at peace with herself, with God and with me. After coming so far in her healing process, she was approachable and open to topics that once caused a great deal of pain. Just having the freedom to talk openly with my mother was liberating in our relationship. I wanted to know more about Giulio and I felt it was finally safe to ask. I wasn't expecting any new information about him; instead, I wanted to rid myself of ill feelings toward him. I didn't want to carry the resentment I felt for him anymore.

Mom and I were about a half-mile down the beach from the rest of the family. We had already found a couple of shells and even a starfish to add to the "great white hunter" competition.

As Mom bent down to pick up another shell, I said, "Mom, can I ask you a question?"

"What's that?"

"It's about Giulio," I said in an easy matter-of-fact tone.

"What about him?" She stood up and we continued walking.

"I've been thinking. It's been 42 years and when I think of him, I feel angry and bitter and I don't want to be angry anymore."

Mom said, "I haven't thought about him in so long. What do you mean, Andrea?"

I tried to explain to Mom, "Well, don't you think it's time for me to forgive him and not have hard feelings toward him? He made a mistake. And we've all made mistakes and by the grace of God, we are where we are today."

Mom listened and seemed to have an agreeable spirit. She made no harsh comments or defensive remarks as she had in the past when I'd mention his name. She just listened in agreement and allowed me to share what was on my heart.

"Mom, I just don't want to be angry with him anymore."

There was silence and then she said very tenderly, "Why would *you* be angry with him?"

"Because he left you—and *me*," I blurted out without hesitation.

I was surprised by her desire to comfort me as she said with a sigh, "Andrea, you have no reason to be angry with him."

Puzzled, I asked, "What do you mean I don't have any reason to be angry with him? He left us."

"Because he came back for you."

I was confused. *"He came back for me?* What do you mean?"

"Yes, he came back for both of us. You see, a month after I told him about my pregnancy, he'd had some time to think. Giulio eventually came back and wanted to marry me. He wanted to take me to Italy to live with his family. Oh, but you know how I am, Andrea, how I used to hold grudges. I was so hurt by his first reaction to the pregnancy and his rejection that I could never forgive him. I was so upset with him that I wanted nothing to do with him ever again. After he rejected me, I cried for weeks and then I cried some more. I made a vow to myself that he would never hurt me again and that I would never trust him again." Her voice was tender as she spoke.

I was stunned. While I listened intently, I was hearing the truth about Giulio for the first time in my life. My world seemed to stop. In the course of five minutes, I learned that my father whom I never knew actually *came back for me*. A feeling of contentment and peace came over me. The realization that I was wanted all along unknowingly exposed the feelings of rejection I never knew existed. I never really felt unwanted until that moment when I heard that I *was* wanted, if that makes any sense.

Suddenly the seashells I carried seemed unimportant. I could no longer hear the sea gulls or the waves. My mind was spinning with emotions—mostly good ones. At the same time, my heart was full of compassion and empathy for my mother. Since I had listened to so many women at the center over the last several years, I had come to understand their feelings of abandonment by the men they loved. I felt a deep sadness for my mother—and for Giulio. I wondered why she hid this from me all my life. But deep inside I knew why. I knew that, in her mind, the risk was too great. It could have meant losing me to the man who had hurt her. As long as I thought Giulio wasn't interested in me, then it was likely I would never want to seek him.

For my mom, it seemed less complicated to just convince herself that he was a bad man and not good for her daughter. I knew she was telling me the truth because she wanted to remove any anger I had in my heart for him. She knew the anger I carried was not warranted and was based on a lie. It was time to set the record straight and be completely honest.

As we continued to walk along the shore and talk, I asked her, "Mom, what about the story you told me of his attempt to kidnap me? Is it possible that he just came to see me?"

"Maybe."

"Of course! It makes more sense now. He didn't come to kidnap me. He came to see me…the child he fathered. To see his daughter that your hurt wouldn't let him be a part of. And the only way was to sneak up a fire escape to get a glimpse of me."

"You're probably right," she said in agreement.

"And because he hurt you, it's only natural you wanted to hurt him back?"

Mom shrugged. It all made sense now. I could understand her hurt and why Mom did what she did. It didn't make it right, but she was 17 and the pain was overwhelming. It was all she knew to do.

I suddenly felt sorry for Giulio. To think, my young, frightened father did want me and came back for me. Giulio was an innocent man all along. I had wrongly accused him of abandoning us. Like my mother, he was scared, too. Giulio was no different from the young men I see every day at the crisis pregnancy center. For these fathers, their world suddenly spins out of control with the news of their girlfriend's unexpected pregnancy, and in an instant they are flooded with questions bigger than themselves. What will he do? How will he support her and the baby? What will her parents think? What will his parents think? He's not ready for this. For some, his first reaction is to run. But in most cases, once the shock of it all wears off, they step up and accept their responsibility, just as Giulio tried to do. He came back with a plan and he came to make things right. He wanted to marry Mom and be a father to me. His resolution was just too late for my mom.

To hear this new revelation from my mother came as a surprise. But I was more surprised that I wasn't angry with her, and instead, understood. I have to give God the credit for that. The compassion I felt for her was because of the work He was doing in my own heart and also because of the timing of her confession. As I look back, I can see God had been preparing me for this for years. That became very clear, as I could see the role the pregnancy center was playing here. Who would have thought the compassion and empathy I have shown to countless clients I would one day offer to my mother concerning her pregnancy with me. It was all a part of His wonderfully ironic plan.

As Mom and I slowly walked back, we occasionally stopped for a shell or for a long stare at the beautiful sunset. Standing there, a little wave washed over my feet gently inviting me to play. I stared at God's splendor and lost myself in wonder. What happens next? Where do I go from here?

The Search for Giulio

It is funny how *one* little detail can change everything. Learning that Giulio did want me and came back for me changed the way I thought of him. I knew instinctively there was only one thing to do and that was to search for him. I needed to hear Giulio's side of the story. I needed to give him the opportunity to know the daughter he fathered, if he still desired to.

The final days of our family vacation afforded me some time of solitude. Long walks along the shore, alone with my thoughts and God, provided a sense of peace and clarity for the next step. Convinced that I needed to search for Giulio, I had conflicting feelings regarding with whom I could share my decision. I wasn't ready to tell Mom or Dad. As open as Mom had been with me, I wasn't entirely sure she would be receptive to me searching for him.

The last thing I ever wanted to do was hurt her or Dad or make them feel they weren't enough for me. I didn't want to tell my husband either. I was afraid Dave would talk me out of it or he would increase the apprehension I already felt about the whole situation. Dave would be concerned that I'd get my hopes up and end up terribly hurt. But after much thought, I decided I'd rather be heartbroken than hold back. It was a risk my heart was willing to take.

However, there were other hesitations that weighed on my mind. I worried that I would disrupt Giulio's life after all these years. What if Giulio had other children? How would they feel about me? Would they question my intentions and think I had ulterior motives? What if he's married and his wife never knew he fathered a child before she came into his life? Would the news be devastating to her? What if I write a letter and it falls into the hands of a family member that would use it to ruin his reputation? What if the letter came back "address unknown"? What if searching for Giulio after 42 years was too late? What if Giulio wasn't even alive and I missed the chance of ever meeting him?

With all of those thoughts running through my head, I knew I needed to talk to someone who knew of Mom and Giulio's past, so I called my Uncle Jonas in Germany. Jonas, my mother's youngest brother, continued to live in Germany after Mom, Donna, and I came to America. He and his wife, Sofia, and my Uncle Romas and Oma all lived in the same town. Over the years, we had kept in contact with letters, phone calls, and, more recently, e-mails. Jonas and Sofia came to the States on two occasions to visit us and stayed six weeks each time. They never had any children of their own.

Jonas is a fascinating man who speaks three languages (German, Italian, and English) and has traveled the world. He was always a long-distance lifeline of support to me, especially in the dark years of Mom's alcohol abuse. Writing letters to him during those days allowed me to vent and safely share my struggles. I always knew that there wasn't much he could do since he lived so far away, but he always encouraged me to "keep my chin up" and not let the circumstances around me define who I was or where I was going. Since he was well acquainted with Mom's background, including her relationship with Giulio, I thought he could offer me some sound advice on whether I should look for Giulio. I made the overseas call, told him my plight, and without hesitation he said, "I think you should search for him, Andrea!"

A Man Without a Name

My next problem was huge. My mother didn't have any written information about Giulio. I didn't have any record of his full name, much less his address. Not even my birth certificate recorded his name as the father. When Mom left Germany, she left all memories and facts about Giulio behind. How was I ever going to locate a man whose last name or address I didn't even know? It's not like I could just Google "Giulio" and find him. Mother had said they met in Germany but that his family lived in Italy. She remembered nothing more than his first name and only recalled his last name "sounded Italian."

As I searched through my important papers, I came across an old letter that the German authorities had sent to me when I was 18 years old. I had kept the document along with my birth certificate, adoption, and naturalization papers.

I remember the day I received the letter. When I came home from school one day, I found the envelope on my bed, which my mother had already opened. It was two pages written in German and I couldn't understand a word of it except for my name and address. It included itemized financial numbers with various dates.

I asked my mother what the letter was all about and she said it was informing me that since I had attained the age of an adult, I was no longer the responsibility of the German government. I asked her what the dollar amounts and dates meant. She said they were child support payments that Giulio was obligated to pay for my benefit. I asked her if I needed to respond. Quite honestly, she tried to translate it but found it difficult since it was written in legal terms. She seemed certain it was nothing more than notification that the case was being closed. Her explanation of the letter satisfied me and I never questioned it again. I just tucked it away with my other important documents.

I realized this old document, which I could have easily thrown away, might be helpful in finding Giulio even though it was 24 years old. The problem was I still couldn't read it. So I decided to find someone who could translate it for me and then I could write to the German agency that sent me the letter and maybe, just maybe, they could tell me something about Giulio and hopefully give me any information they had on file. I contacted a German professor at the local community college and arranged a meeting with him. Professor Hansen was willing to translate the letter for me and give me any advice he could.

In Black and White

The day I met with Professor Hansen was like God parting the Red Sea for me. As the professor read the letter line by line, he translated it to me. Within a few minutes,

I understood what the document was saying. Mother was right about most of it. The government was closing my case concerning any custody issues. But, according to that letter, Giulio *did* pay child support until Dad adopted me three years later. Mom never told me that.

As the professor continued through the letter, he matter-of-factly read Giulio's name—his first name and last name. Then he read his address.

"What was that?" I asked.

"Giulio..." the professor began.

In mid-sentence, I interrupted, "Did you just say Giulio's full name and address?"

"Uh...yeah, that's what it says."

His name and address were in the letter, right there in black and white in front of my eyes. I had his address all along! How could I have missed it? Truth is anyone could have missed it. Nothing made sense looking at this foreign legal document. The spelling of his name and the style of the letter were so unusual. It was like looking at a million alphabet letters all mixed up. His name just blended in with the other German letters. I couldn't make out a single word. The punctuation and lower case letters were different, too, not allowing anything to stand out. I would have never seen it. But there it was—his name and last known address in a region of northern Italy. Now I had something to work with. I would start the search with the name and address printed on that old document. Keeping in mind, this letter was sent to me when I was 18, but the custody case was actually filed in 1963. There was a possibility that the address listed was over 40 years old.

A Message in a Bottle

Now I had his full name and address and still Jonas was the only other person who knew what I was up to. I wanted to scream and tell everyone, but I didn't dare. I would tell the rest of my family after the letter was in the mail.

First, I had to write the letter. What did I want to say? I certainly didn't want to sound desperate or scare Giulio off. I needed to assure him that I had no ulterior motive and that I wasn't interested in an inheritance or payment of any kind. I just wanted to meet him and ask if he was interested in having any contact with me. Ultimately, the letter would be brief, direct, and unemotional.

Then I got to thinking. What are the chances that Giulio lived in the same place after all these years? What if the letter is returned or sits on some Italian postal shelf for a long time and then gets scrapped? Then I thought maybe the residents of the address would know of Giulio and forward the letter to him. I held on to the whole idea very loosely that Giulio would ever get the letter. The chances were very slim and with all things considered, I composed a very simple letter.

Dear Mr. Giulio De Luca:

My name is Andrea Dagmar Marciulaytite Krazeise. My mother's name is Erika Maria Marciulaytite. I was born in Ulm, Germany in 1963. My mother and I left Germany in 1966 and we now live in Florida, USA.

The purpose of this letter is to search for my biological father. According to a German document that was sent to me when I was 18 years old, your name, Giulio De Luca, is recorded as my biological father. It is my wish to make your acquaintance, if you are interested.

It is not my desire or motive to request anything of you. I would simply like to know if you would like to meet me. It is not my intention to hurt you or your family, therefore I would understand if this request cannot be granted.

If you are interested, please contact me.

Sincerely,
Andrea Krazeise

I ended it with my phone number, address, e-mail address, and fax number. I stuffed the letter and a small family photo into a plain white envelope, addressed it, walked to the end of my driveway and opened the mailbox. Not knowing whose hands it would reach or if it would get lost, I kissed the envelope and prayed, *"Lord, if it's your will, let this letter beat all odds and be received by Giulio, alive and well."* Then I put it in the mailbox like any other first-class mail. No extra postage, no express mail—just regular postal delivery to the last known address. And I thought, what did I have to lose?

Chapter Thirteen

No Turning Back

O nce the letter was signed, sealed and on its way across the Atlantic, it was safe to tell Dave. I wasn't in the habit of keeping things from him and my covert actions were causing me some anxiety. I told him the moment he came home from work. He wasn't surprised and he gave me that knowing smile that told me deep down he was glad I did. Hearing the truth about Giulio during our vacation had come as a shock to him, too. "I knew you'd do this and I'm glad you did it. But you know, Andrea, there's a real possibility that nothing will come of this," Dave said. Deep down I knew that, too, and was fully prepared to accept whatever happened. At least I wouldn't have any regrets for not trying.

I also needed to let my parents know, so I made a visit to their house to tell them in person. To my surprise and relief, they were both very supportive and gave me their blessings. Dad comforted me by saying, "Andrea, it's a good thing that you sent the letter. You have every right to meet him, and he is probably a good man."

A Message From...

It was exactly ten days from the day I sent the letter that I received the most shocking and unexpected news. Our family came home from church one ordinary Sunday to find the message light blinking on the phone. As Dave, the kids, and I all bustled around in the kitchen, Kate played the message. Within seconds, we all stood frozen, listening to a foreign man's voice. "Who's that, Mommy?" Kate asked, as we were all confused. It couldn't be Giulio. The letter was sent just days ago. After we quieted everyone down, I pushed the "play" button again to carefully listen to the voice of the man speaking.

I had no idea what he was saying. I couldn't tell if he was happy or angry. I thought he sounded nervous—or was it passion I heard in his voice? The message was approximately 50 seconds long and at the end I recognized only two words, "*Ciao, Andrea.*" Then I knew it was Italian. I played it again. Could it be him? Or was it someone else who received the letter and felt obliged to call me? Could it be one of Giulio's relatives telling me that he was dead? Or was it one of Giulio's sons telling me to get lost?

"How are you going to get that translated?" Dave asked me. As I paced the kitchen floor, I started to panic. I needed someone to translate the message now! I called several people to ask for their suggestions. Then it dawned on me. I remembered a friend from church that very morning introducing me to her Italian father who was visiting from New York. Could he speak or understand Italian? I knew it was a long shot. I mean just because someone is Italian and likes spaghetti doesn't mean he can *speak* Italian.

I tracked her down and found out that indeed he did speak Italian. Hallelujah! My friend and her father were at my house 45 minutes later. Before listening to the message, I explained the somewhat unusual circumstances of this call and who the caller might be. We all gathered around the telephone. Dave was standing next to me. He grabbed my hand and squeezed it. I took a deep breath and pushed the "play" button. My eyes were locked on the translator. My heart was beating so hard that I could hear my pulse in my ears. I prayed silently, *"O God, please let it be Giulio!"*

I watched the translator's face looking for some sign to indicate whether it was good news or bad, but I couldn't read his expression. He just stared intently at the machine as he listened. Finally, after many long agonizing seconds, he looked up at me and smiled. Then he translated the sweetest message I've ever heard: *"Buon giorno, mia cara!"* which means, "Greetings, my beloved!" It was Giulio! He told us he was bursting with joy and excitement to have received my letter. I screamed with delight and started jumping around the kitchen. I wanted to hear the translation over and over so that I could memorize every word of it. My dear interpreter finally wrote down the whole message word for word.

Giulio explained that he would send me a letter soon, but he was undergoing minor surgery the following day and asked that I be patient. He promised he would begin writing as soon as he got home from the hospital. I was so happy to hear that he wanted to write me. Oh, how I wished Giulio had left his phone number on the message, so we could have called him back.

After my friend and her father left, I listened to the message over and over. I wanted to hear Giulio's voice and try to match his words to the written words I had on paper. I wished I knew what kind of surgery he was having. I prayed to God for Giulio's protection and not to let anything happen to him. Wouldn't it be a cruel irony if he was seriously ill and I ended up the victim of a cosmic joke?

I decided to call my mother to tell her the news since she already knew about the letter. She was very surprised that I had actually heard from him and she wanted to hear it for herself. Within an hour, she and Dad were in my kitchen listening to the message I practically had memorized by then. As she listened, she looked at me and chuckled, "Yes! That's Giulio!" Then she handed me several baby photos of me that she dug out before coming and suggested I send them to him.

I floated on a cloud for days. I couldn't stop smiling thinking how a letter sent to an old address across the ocean reached the doorstep of my father—and he called me right away! I wondered if he was just as anxious about meeting me. Was he married and did he have children? The phone call was so brief and seemed like a tease to the many questions I wanted to ask.

For days, we left the message on the machine and I must have played it three or four times a day. It was so satisfying to hear his voice. It was the only connection I had with Giulio and I couldn't bear to erase it.

Special Delivery

Hardly more than a week passed and the eagerly awaited letter from Giulio arrived. There it was in the mailbox, a highly significant piece of mail lying casually between some junk mail. I wondered if the postman had any idea what he had just delivered to me. This precious letter had traveled thousands of miles across the Atlantic Ocean to find me. It contained the handwritten words of the man who fathered me 42 years ago and who did, in fact, *come back for me*.

I imagined him sitting at his desk in Italy, folding the paper, sliding it into the envelope and sealing the letter with the DNA we shared. I studied his handwriting and how he wrote my name on the outside of the envelope. I wanted to savor every part of the letter. I then held the letter close to my chest as I walked up the driveway to the house. I headed straight to the kitchen to grab my favorite paring knife. This was no ordinary letter to be torn apart. This one required a clean slice so I could save it forever.

It was a two-page letter on plain white paper printed in Italian. For the next three hours, I painstakingly translated his handwritten letter. Word by word, I used an online translation website to interpret the words he wanted to convey. Translating the letter was harder than I expected. It was difficult to determine if a letter was an "m" or "u." Was that lettering an "a" or "d"? If I misspelled the word, I couldn't get a translation. It was the word puzzle of a lifetime and every word successfully decoded was a victory. When I finally finished, it read:

Dear Andrea,

 I have received your letter. I am amazed, stunned and very happy. You have a big beautiful family. I hope you are very happy. You are very beautiful. In the letter, you have only told me a little about everything. When did you leave for America? Where did you meet your husband? Why did you wait all these years to come to me? I am 64 years old and have a few health problems. Fifteen years ago, it would have been possible to come and visit if you wanted and desired it. Dear Andrea, if you could answer, I ask you please tell me about your mother. You have to believe me and not be angry. Because of my medical treatments, I have lost some of my memory. After 42 years, I do not remember your mother's name. I do not take the blame off me, but did she use a different name? For sure I would have known her under a different name. I wish you a lot of happiness. I embrace you and all your splendid family. I am married to Camile, she is 60 years old. We have three daughters, which would

*be your half-sisters—Carla age 40, Viviana age 35
and Bianca age 31.*
   Please write me back very soon.
      Giulio

My heart was so full. Giulio was embracing me and my
family and he was open to having continued contact with
me. Learning that I had three half-sisters was exciting. I
loved my sister Donna and to think I had three more was like
winning the "sister lottery." The idea of being a part of a big
family was thrilling. I wondered if we looked alike. Donna
and I were as opposite as night and day. She was blonde with
hazel green eyes, while I was a brunette with dark brown
eyes. Donna always looked like a California beach girl
with golden skin and striking eyes. We were both married
with kids, so I wondered if my other sisters were, too. What
kinds of things did they like to do? So many questions rolled
through my mind. How I longed to see a photo of Giulio and
his daughters, to see if we shared any family resemblance.

It was apparent from his letter that he had genuine questions that deserved truthful answers. I owed it to him to
explain everything since it wasn't his choice that Mother
and I left Germany and that he never saw me again. When he
asked, "Why did you wait all these years to come for me?"
my heart ached for the years he lost. I felt he deserved the
truth—even about the dark days of my life and why it took
me 42 years to find him. I would have to tell him of my mother's alcohol abuse, her recovery and our healed relationship
that led to these recent times in order for him to understand
why I never contacted him over the years. Reading the tone
of his letter, I also wanted to assure him I was not dwelling
on the missed years that we were denied and instead wanted
to celebrate the time we did have.

The following day, I wrote him a six-page letter and
explained everything. I could have easily written a book but

I didn't want to burden him with every single detail. There was so much to tell him. I began with my mother's story and the course she chose after coming to America. I tried to find the right words to explain she hadn't painted the kindest picture of him. Somehow I had to make him understand that for almost four decades, she harbored so much hurt and anger that any mention of his name set her off. Because of her wounded heart, any conversation about him had always been off limits—until just two months ago.

I explained it was only because of a recent conversation Mother and I had on our beach vacation where she confessed the truth about him which motivated me to search for him. I also explained that it was only a few weeks ago that I had discovered his full name and address. As I wrote, I wondered if his feelings had been hurt by my silence all these years. Trying to imagine myself in his shoes was painful.

Two weeks later, I received another letter from Giulio. He was thankful for the long letter and all that I shared. In his letter, he explained that his wife, Camile, knew about me before they were married. She remembered the child support payments that he sent to my mother in the early years. I was encouraged to hear she understood and that she admired my courage for searching for him after all these years.

He continued to explain the reason he actually left Italy to come to Germany was for a job waiting for him in Kempton, Germany. During his travels to Kempton, he stopped in Ulm where my mother lived for a meal in the Italian restaurant, Napoli's. While he was enjoying his meal, he overheard the owner fire the cook and then in a later conversation with Giulio the owner offered the cook's position to him. The original job in Kempton would have to wait.

During his time in Ulm is when Giulio met my mother and fathered me. Once my mother and I left Germany for America, almost four years later, Giulio resumed his journey to Kempton, where he later met Camile. Interestingly, Camile faced a similar situation as mine. Coming from Italy herself, she was in Kempton for the sole purpose of searching for her own father, a German soldier she never met. She was 20 years old when her search led to her father's hometown of Kempton. Camile never found her biological father, but it was there she met Giulio.

Camile's family lived in northern Italy, while Giulio's family came from southern Italy. Giulio and Camile fell in love, married and had their first child, Carla, and within a few years, they all moved back to Italy to Camile's home-town and settled into their own place.

In Giulio's letter, he explained that his daughters did not know about me. He said that he was waiting for many answers from me before he shared the news with them. Giulio asked me to be patient, as he needed to wait for the right time. He wasn't sure how they would react to the news of having a half-sister in America. His greatest concern was for his middle daughter, Viviana. He feared that she would not take the news very well.

Viviana was deeply attached to her father and Giulio was afraid that she might feel threatened or jealous of me. She had health issues that included battling kidney disease. He was naturally a concerned father and worried that the news would cause some anxiety in the family. Giulio and Camile wanted to embrace me into their family, but the timing of the news was important.

Hearing all of that made me feel heavy-hearted. That was not my intent. The last thing I wanted to do was upset his family. I wrote to him again and reminded him that I had no selfish motive or agenda and I certainly didn't want to come between him and his daughters. They didn't deserve that. I told him I understood his position and that his loyalty had to be to his three daughters. I tried to read between the lines in his letters to understand things fully, but because of the long-distance communication and trouble translating every word, it made our exchange difficult. It would have been so much easier to sit down face to face and talk through it all, but that was not possible.

For the next two months, Giulio and I continued to write one another, and in his third letter, he enclosed a small photo of himself. It looked like an old passport picture, very small. But it was beautiful and I studied it for hours, looking for a resemblance. We had similarities in our nose and chin. We both had almond-shaped eyes and a slight dimple in our chin. He had warm eyes, a gentle smile and was very handsome. I got the impression that he was a quiet man. His letters were full of endearments and signed with "many kisses to my grandchildren." However, I continued to be anxious about my three sisters and their reaction to me. When was he going to tell them? How long would I have to wait? Would their reaction change the course of our newfound relationship?

The News Hits the Fan

One morning, about a month later, my husband woke me up with the news that we had an e-mail from Viviana. "Viviana! What did she say?" I shouted as I jumped out of bed, grabbing for my bathrobe.

"I don't know. It's in Italian and I don't read Italian— yet," Dave said with a hint of sarcasm.

I ran to the computer to see the e-mail. I opened the letter and saw the text was in Italian. I quickly searched for an online translation website to which I could cut and paste the text. I was so nervous and jittery, I had to remind myself to breathe. Within minutes, I was reading her first e-mail. The translation was very rough.

Hi Andrea, I am Viviana, one of the daughters of Papa Giulio.

How strange to find myself writing to a person whom I do not know, who came into my life in a very strange and sudden way. I do not know how to control my emotions. On Sunday, March 19th, I became aware of your existence as a sister of mine. I will not deny that I feel confused and betrayed. Although at the same time I want to get to know you. But, I do need some time. I have only learned of you this past week. Unlike you, from what I understand from your letters, you have known forever. Therefore, you are more prepared than I am to deal with these sorts of feelings. It is right that you and papa should meet. I support this idea, but at the same time, I feel strange calling you my sister. Therefore, have patience and give me time to get used to the idea that you even exist.

I consider myself a very direct person. One who says what she thinks, but I need to cover all bases in order to live securely. This news, though, has really thrown me. My father, also your father, let's just say Papa Giulio, he tells me that you would like to have contact with us some day. What is your livelihood Andrea? If you can tell me something about your mother, Erika, and how she and Papa met, I would be very glad to try and understand the situation better. Don't call me nosy or invading, but it seems legiti-mate to ask you these questions since I don't really know who you are, even though you are my sister, at least since March 19th, 2006. As for me, you were born on that day. Please don't take this as an offense, because that is not how I mean it. You might read me as being a little confused, but that is what I am right now. I have a thousand emotions. I don't want you to

*think badly of me. That is not my intention. I swear,
that is not my motive. I hope this e-mail is clear and
legible when you receive it. I will be waiting for news
from you.*
  Viviana

Somewhat stunned and unsure how to take all that, I swallowed the big lump in my throat and thought, "Wow! She is surely direct and doesn't mince words." For the most part, I was relieved and appreciated her honesty. I was thankful, too. I mean, it could have been a lot worse. One thing for sure, I knew my response to her letter would require that I weigh out each word very carefully, allowing her time to process it all. I prayed that God would help me convey a tender and truthful reply. The last thing I wanted to do was upset her. So much was at stake and I was painfully aware that I needed Viviana's approval if a future reunion with Giulio was ever to take place.

In my desperation, I prayed, *"Lord! Help me be patient with her and help me ease her anxieties. I don't want to say anything stupid."* I wanted her to know that I understood her position and I was not going to hurt her. She needed assurance of my willingness to discontinue any further contact with the family if that would make her feel better. To gain her trust was essential. Had I been in her shoes I probably would have felt the same way.

In that first week of e-mails, God was working on Viviana's heart. Our two and three e-mails daily became warmer and warmer as the week went by. I was beginning to see signs of her opening up to me and sharing some of her fears and concerns. Her salutations eventually went from "Viviana" to "Vivi" and then to "Love, Vivi" and that seemed like a huge victory. I was encouraged by the direction we were heading. She raised many questions about Giulio and my mother's acquaintance. She wanted to know more about the validity of Giulio being my birth father. I responded quickly to each of her e-mails and shared in detail everything I knew. Within a week, she came to understand it all.

To my surprise, Viviana showed empathy for my mother's plight and expressed compassion toward her. She understood that our parents were young and made mistakes. She seemed to understand the power of grace and forgiveness and alluded to some mistakes she had made in her life as well.

Getting acquainted with Carla and Bianca came much easier. About three days after receiving Viviana's first e-mail, I received an e-mail from Carla and Bianca. Both of their letters were very encouraging and understanding. They both explained that I was a "big surprise," but they were open-minded and eager to meet me. I felt a great sense of relief about their openness to welcome me into their lives.

Over the next few weeks, all three of my half-sisters were e-mailing me often and I was busy addressing each sister separately, as they all had different questions and perspectives. They all were interested in forming a new relationship with their half-sister. The best days were opening the e-mails to find photos of themselves and the men in their lives. Our resemblance was undeniable. I could see physical traits in them that we shared. Bianca and I had the same eyes. Carla and I had the same smile. Viviana and I had the same facial structure. It was fascinating to learn about their lives, interests, passions, and feelings toward me and even their own relationships with our father.

Each Sister Unique

Viviana was the middle sister of the three. She and Nico had been married seven years. He was a carpenter by trade and played on a championship soccer team. She attended all of his games and was his biggest cheerleader. They owned their own villa in the town next to Giulio. During the soccer off-season, Nico liked to renovate their home. Viviana was a teacher's aide in a preschool and loved working with children. Because of her kidney disease, she was unable to have children of her own. Fascinated by my work at the crisis pregnancy center, she talked freely about her frustration with those who could conceive yet would terminate their pregnancy, when she longed for a child of her own. Viviana was into reading the stars and astrology. It struck me odd that one of her first personal questions for me was what my sign was. I call Viviana my "Star Gazing" sister.

Carla was the oldest following me. She graduated from college with a degree in philosophy. She and Stefano had been together for 13 years after finding each other through some political involvement at a time when he served as the town's mayor. They were both very interested in politics and nature. Carla worked in an international gift shop in a small neighboring city. It was a congested city devoted to business, culture, and the arts. The shop she managed carried items from various countries and tribes such as jewelry, clothing, baskets, food, spices, handmade soaps and other things. I found it very interesting that all the proceeds generated went to support Amnesty International. Fashion and material things were not important to Carla. Her passion was taking care of less fortunate people in third-world countries and the environment. I affectionately refer to her as my "Green Peace" sister.

Bianca, the youngest of the three, lived in the same city as Carla. It appeared that she and Carla were very close. Bianca is my "Super Model" sister. She is tall, beautiful, and loves fashion. Giovanni and Bianca had been together for three years and were making plans to marry. Giovanni was a handsome, affluent businessman and loved fine wine, custom-tailored clothes and his beautiful Bianca.

Bianca's career choice was most intriguing to me. She was the president of a non-profit organization that educated and found employment opportunities for physically and mentally handicapped individuals, providing them dignity and independence. This organization produced stationery products like photo albums, frames, cards, fancy gift boxes and more. They offered meaningful employment and housing for over 100 people. Each person had a task according to their skill, with consideration of their limitations, enabling them to become productive citizens. Bianca shared that as a young girl she liked to volunteer at a local handicap facility. Years later, she learned of this organization and went to work for them. After a few years, the board of directors appointed her as president and as their spokeswoman.

It didn't take long to recognize the common thread that the four of us shared. The same bloodline wasn't the only thing we had in common. My heart burst with pride hearing their passions and the fact we all possessed hearts to serve. As I was getting acquainted with them, they wanted to know all about what I did at the Sanford Crisis Pregnancy Center and how it got started. They were intrigued by what life was like in America and my life as a mother. Each one shared her desire to have children of her own. To learn they now have two nephews and a niece was exciting news for them. They wanted to know about the foods I liked, my hobbies, the style of our home, and the kind of flowers growing in my garden. Gladly I shared it all…three times!

Each sister described her relationship with Giulio. Viviana was clearly the closest to him and very protective. They told me that Giulio was a quiet man who kept his thoughts to himself. It was often difficult for them, as they wanted him to be more open and express his emotions freely. Giulio and Camile were in the restaurant business until he retired three years ago. Throughout his life, he had owned three restaurants. His reputation described him as the best pizza maker in town. Their menu included the typical authentic Italian fare like pasta, sauces, pizza, calzones, and salads. Every day had been spent in the restaurant. They were not rich but owned a nice three-bedroom flat and lived comfortably.

My sisters mentioned that their father seemed to miss his work. Retirement had not been an easy transition for Giulio. Due to some health condition and the stress of the restaurant business, everyone thought it best if he retired. With not having a job to go to and his health issues, he was becoming somewhat depressed. Carla said that the news of me "was like spring time for him" and that there was a noticeable spark in his mood.

Plans Made

Once I shared the news with my Uncle Jonas in Germany of making contact with Giulio, he helped me with the translation of important information. He began having dialogue with Giulio over the phone and they became acquainted as well. Since Uncle Jonas spoke Italian and English he was eager to help convey some of my messages to Giulio.

Within a few months, Giulio and Uncle Jonas were discussing the idea and details of a future face-to-face visit. Giulio invited me, Dave, and our children to come for an official family reunion in Italy. He also invited Uncle Jonas and Aunt Sofia. They were happy to come along and Jonas agreed to serve as the family translator. It was reassuring to know that he would be with me every step of the way.

We set a date of June 26, 2007. The trip would include Dave, Kate, and me. Our boys chose to stay home. David was working at his intern position in sports medicine during the summer and Daniel wanted to attend summer camp with his best friend. Giulio and Uncle Jonas had it all planned. Dave, Kate, and I would arrive in Germany first, stay a few days, and then travel by car to Italy with Uncle Jonas and

Aunt Sofia. We would spend the first three nights in Giulio's home and visit his town. Then the entire family, all 13 of us, would stay a week in a beach house an hour away from Venice. Our family reunion in Italy would be a total of ten days.

We purchased our tickets five months prior to the trip and watched the days tick slowly off the calendar. Anticipation mounted and my curiosity and imagination raced out of control. It was very difficult for me to keep my mind focused on the present knowing that God was preparing something awesome — just for me. I had waited a lifetime. Now it proved hard to wait a few more months.

Chapter 14

A Family Reunion Unfolds

"PLEASE FASTEN YOUR SEATBELTS! It's time to prepare the cabin for landing." The flight attendant's voice over the intercom stirred me from my fitful sleep. I couldn't help but wonder if I was in for a bumpy landing or the ride of my life. I almost had to pinch myself. I was fully aware that I never could have orchestrated what was taking place. God had been weaving this tapestry for generations and now one more cord was about to be woven into place.

We were just minutes away from being greeted by Uncle Jonas and Aunt Sofia at the Stuttgart Airport. We would stay at their house over the weekend so I could spend a few days with my grandmother, Oma, and visit my hometown. As we came out of the airport terminal, we heard an enthusiastic voice calling, "Andrea! Over here!" Uncle Jonas and Aunt Sofia were waving fervently to get our attention. They were just as excited as we were about the journey we were about to make together.

Within hours of our arrival, we gathered around Oma's table for an authentic German meal she had fussed over all day. Oma was so happy to see us, and for the first time, she met her great-granddaughter, Kate. Since the time I left Germany at age four, I had been back only once. About

14 years earlier, I made a visit with our oldest son, David. Oma had been to see us twice, staying for several weeks at a time, so we weren't really strangers and even talked like old friends (with Jonas' help interpreting).

The evening was full of laughs and hugs and our bellies were full of potato balls. When Oma came to the States to visit us, she commandeered my kitchen and made potato balls for us because she knew how much I liked them. As I watched my 87-year-old grandmother, it was hard to believe she once encountered Adolph Hitler in a factory she worked in as a young woman. She still lived in the same government-subsidized apartment that she moved into after the days of the DP camp. It was the place where Mother and I lived before we left for America.

Though it was old, her apartment was bright, inviting, and very comfortable. It reminded me of the way Mom decorated our house when I was a young girl. There were plenty of fresh flowers in jars. Lace curtains swayed in the breeze, and crocheted pillows were nestled on the couch. Neatly arranged knick-knacks decorated her bookshelves and her walls displayed dozens of photos that I had sent over the years.

After dinner, I casually toured all the rooms in her apartment, taking in each one and enjoying every detail. I was most fascinated with the room that once had been my bedroom. It had been converted into a little television room where Oma liked to sew. As I stood looking at all the photos, many of them were of me as a baby. I tried to imagine my nursery. Walking around the room, I thought about what it must have felt like the day Mother brought me home from the hospital and envisioned her holding me, and feeling overwhelmed. As I continued to walk around the room, I was drawn to the window that looked out to the courtyard. For the first time in my life, I noticed the fire escape. My heart melted. That was the very place Giulio had stood to get a glimpse of me in my crib—before my mother ran him off. Speechless, I stood in awe.

I chuckled at the thought of what life would have been like today if he really had kidnapped me like she said. Of course, he wasn't ever going to abduct me. He just wanted to see his baby. The thought of seeing him face to face in a matter of days was almost overwhelming.

Later, we left Oma's house and went to Uncle Jonas's home to relax and unpack. As Dave, Kate, and I were getting cleaned up, the phone rang. I heard Uncle Jonas talking and laughing. Within seconds, Jonas shouted, "Andrea, come here!"

He handed me the phone. "It's Giulio!" My heart skipped a beat. All I could say was, *"buon giorno!"*

Giulio had managed to learn a sentence or two in English and asked, "Andrea, how are you? I am happy to see you soon! I love you!" It had been over a year since he first called me and left that unexpected message on my answering machine. I was overjoyed to hear his voice again. I don't know who was more excited, him or me.

After a minute of exchanging more comments that neither of us understood, Uncle Jonas came to my rescue. I couldn't believe it was really going to happen. As Jonas and Giulio talked and discussed the details of our arrival, my heart danced with joy. Dave and Kate and I hugged and kissed each other with sheer excitement. How in the world would we ever get to sleep that night? But since we'd had a big day, sleep was not hard to find. The moment our tired little heads hit our pillows, we were out.

Over the next few days, we spent time with Oma and my other uncle, Romas, and his wife, Brigette. Our conversations with family were full and lively. There was so much to talk about. Oma and my uncles wanted to know everything about our lives in America. There was lots of discussion about my mom and dad as well. They were happy to hear about their recovery and the new lives they were enjoying. Jonas and Romas urged me to convince my mother to come back for a visit. Mom had never been back to Germany after she left in 1966. Somehow, I had to make her realize that Oma would not live forever and her brothers longed to see her again.

During our four days in Germany, we did the tourist thing and visited a Bavarian castle, the beautiful Munster cathedral in Ulm, and a wildlife sanctuary near Salem. But as exciting as those days were, they still seemed to drag. The only thing I had on my mind was getting to Italy and meeting Giulio face to face.

The Longest Drive of My Life

The day finally came to leave for Italy. We were up by 5 a.m. and in the car by 7 a.m., with Uncle Jonas and Aunt Sofia in the front seat and the three of us in the back. Uncle Jonas and my husband had the trip all planned out. Their best guess was that the trip would take between six and eight hours. That didn't seem like much—a day at work or a good night's sleep—but to me, it was an eternity.

The first hour of the trip passed quickly. We were giddy and chatty. By the third hour, I was convinced the clock was going backward. We listened to American songs on the radio and Uncle Jonas provided a little comic relief. He had a great sense of humor and at times broke the silence by giving us his rendition of our popular tunes. Of course, we laughed and had some fun at his expense. Then there were times when Uncle Jonas, sensing my anxiety, simply looked at me in his rearview mirror with a warm smile.

Uncle Jonas was just as excited as I was. We were all experiencing a nervous energy. At one point, I got the bright idea that if I took my watch off, the minutes would go faster. I consciously tried to focus elsewhere. The breathtaking scenery helped. Driving through Austria and watching the

Alps roll by was awesome. God really outdid Himself when He created that panorama. Dave enjoyed the view with me but wasn't very talkative because he was listening to his iPod. Kate was engrossed in her handheld video game.

I'm not sure where we were when my nervous energy and giddiness turned the corner to connect me with the God of all creation. It might have been the scenery or maybe it was the realization that He was smiling about what was up ahead. My thoughts and silent prayers kept me occupied. As I spoke to God, I thanked Him over and over. I was just hours away from meeting my father. It didn't seem that long ago that I was counting months, then weeks, then days—but now it was only hours.

Here was my uncle traveling by my side as my Italian translator. Did he ever imagine as a little boy, the Catholic boarding school he attended in Italy and the Italian he learned to speak would one day translate the words spoken between Giulio and me?

And what about the letter that was sent to Giulio? It was a miracle that it even arrived considering the only address I had was almost 40 years old. The fact that I kept that German document was nothing short of amazing. That was the only connection I had with Giulio's full name and address. God's timing of my mother's truthful revelation and how Giulio came back for me was just another piece in the beautiful puzzle.

So much had happened. My mind began flashing back to so many scenes of my life. Dad being coaxed into going to AA meetings and then Mom and Dad's recovery from alcohol, which led to my mother's healing and her amends to me. Then God called me into the ministry, which prepared me to hear Mom's confession about Giulio on the shores of Longboat Key. All of these scenes plus several more raced through my mind. In hindsight, I can see that if one single event had been left out, I would not be heading toward this most joyous meeting. There was nothing random about the events in my life. They all brought me to this moment. My heart was (and still is) full of gratitude.

My deepest thoughts were interrupted when Uncle Jonas said, "Are we ready to stop for some lunch?" It was about noon. We were only halfway there. We desperately needed to stretch, refuel, and refresh. While everyone had a hearty appetite, I was restless. Even half of a sandwich seemed to stick in my throat. Once we got back into the car, I was desperate to get my mind off counting the minutes, so I commandeered Kate's Game Boy and attempted to play *Mario Cart*.

Two hours later, Jonas announced, "Three more miles!" Giulio lived in the northern region of Italy and we were already there. My heart skipped a beat. Did I hear that right? I figured we still had hours to go. Instantly, I became nervous and my stomach started to churn. My shoulders tightened up and my hands began to sweat. In a panic, I reapplied my lipstick and freshened up. Jonas had a navigation system in his car and we began to hear more frequent commands from the dashboard, "Turn left. Turn right. In one mile turn right. Your destination is two miles on the right."

The Man I'd Soon Call Papa Giulio

Jonas called Giulio from his cell phone to let him know we were just minutes away. We made better time than we had expected. We were about two hours early. Giulio was delighted to know we were just a few miles from his house. He told Jonas he would be outside at the end of his street waiting for us. A rain shower approached and a light mist began to fall—nothing heavy, but enough to put the windshield wipers on. Captivated by the old world scenery spread out before us, we drove through the little village. I watched people go in and out of bakeries and cafes along the narrow brick streets. Linens waved on balcony clotheslines and herb gardens hung from windowsills. It all seemed so surreal. And we were just seconds away from seeing Giulio.

Suddenly, thoughts began running through my head. *"Are we in the right town? Is this the right house? Is this man, Giulio, really my father?"* I quickly asked, "Jonas, will you recognize him when you see him? It's been so many years...exactly how will you know if it's him?"

"I don't think I will have any problem with that, Andrea." Somehow, even his calm and reassuring voice did little to quiet my doubts.

"There he is!" said Jonas. We saw him before he saw us. He was standing beside his car holding an umbrella. "That's Giulio! I recognize him. That's your father, Andrea!"

My insides were screaming with intense emotions. The next few minutes seemed like a slow-motion film. We drove toward him, parked the car, opened the doors and slowly stepped out. Giulio walked toward the driver's side of the car and greeted Jonas first. As they exchanged a handshake, Dave and Kate and I came around the front of the car. Dave, Jonas, and Sofia all stepped aside.

Time stood still. At 44 years of age, I stood before my father as we met face to face. We moved toward each other quickly. The embrace was unforgettable. Over and over he said my name—with his Italian accent. My name never sounded so sweet. *"Andrea, Andrea, mia Andrea!"* I tried to take in every detail during that first hug. I felt his aging body. He was tall, thin, and smelled like fresh aftershave. Standing under an umbrella with the majestic Italian Alps as a backdrop, I embraced the man I would now call 'Papa Giulio.' When I finally pulled away to wipe my tears, he studied my face. He held my chin in his hands and kissed me on each cheek and then hugged me again. I felt like a little girl in his arms.

The tears flowed freely. I motioned for Dave and Kate to step forward. My father embraced Dave with a hearty hug and strong pats on the back. Over Dave's shoulder, Giulio saw Kate and moved toward her. He kneeled down and held my little girl by her shoulders to study her. She was his first grandchild he would behold. He ran his fingers through her silky blonde hair and marveled at her big blue eyes. *"Bellissima! Bellissima, mia cara Kate!"* He wrapped his arms around her tiny seven-year-old frame.

Within minutes, our little group moved inside his house. He and Camile lived on the second floor of an apartment-style flat. It was a beautiful place. There were balconies on each side to enjoy the glorious view of the town and mountains. The windows were open to allow in the fresh mountain air.

When the door to their kitchen opened, the scent of olive oil mixed with garlic and fresh herbs filled the rooms. Camile was there to greet us with hugs and kisses. She was an attractive lady with short, wavy gray hair and blazing blue eyes. She had a towel over her shoulder and was busy cooking our first family meal. Embracing each of us, Camile apologized for still having her apron on. It was about 3:00 in the afternoon and the rest of the family was not expected until 6:00. Arriving earlier than we expected, we relaxed in their living room and nibbled on prosciutto, cheese, cantaloupe slices, and wine. Without hesitation, we began getting acquainted.

There was one thing I had to do before my sisters arrived. I had a special gift for Papa Giulio. I had made a scrapbook for him. In the months prior to our trip, I had collected pictures that told the story of my life. Because he had missed so much, I wanted to share snapshots of my life with him in this special album. I included over four decades of photos, beginning with me as a baby, then pictures of me in elementary school, ballet class, graduation from high school, and my wedding. I dedicated five or six pages to each of his three grandchildren. I included photos from their baby days to current shots so he could see them as they've grown. There were pictures of our home, pets, the pregnancy center, some of our vacations and even flowers from my garden. I had each page carefully matted and labeled for him. I was eager to present it to him.

As I sat next to him, he carefully unwrapped the album. The look on his face said more than words could express. "Andrea! Andrea! How beautiful!" He opened the first page and saw three black-and-white photos of me at 12 months. It was a series of photographs that Mother had done by a photography studio while we still lived in Germany.

Suddenly, he became very emotional and animated as he looked at those three particular pictures. He spoke to Jonas, saying things I could not understand. By the look on Jonas' face, I knew something was about to happen. Papa Giulio had made some kind of connection. He quickly got up from his chair and went to their china cabinet. He pulled out his own family photo album and brought it to where we were sitting. Hastily, he fumbled through the pages, as if he were purposely looking for something. I didn't understand what he was doing, so I looked at Jonas pleadingly, "What's going on?"

Jonas held up his finger, "Just wait, Andrea. He's looking for something." As Papa Giulio nervously flipped the pages, I briefly caught glimpses of baby photos of Carla, Viviana, and Bianca. I figured that maybe he was looking for a photo to compare our resemblance. Then he found what he was looking for. With a sigh, he held a five-by-seven-inch photograph against his chest and then handed it to me. I was stunned to see that it was a picture of me. Papa Giulio handed me the exact same baby picture that was on the first page of the album I made for him. He said something and Jonas told me, "That is a picture your mother gave him before you left Germany." He had kept my baby picture all those years. Now I was the one who was speechless and all choked up.

It was in that moment that I realized I *was* in the right house with the right man...and this was God's perfect timing.

During the next couple of hours, they played Italian music on an old record player. Camile was a lively, fun woman and waltzed around the room with Kate as the music played. Between dances, Camile and Papa Giulio were in and out of the kitchen preparing the feast we going to share once the rest of the family arrived. The smell of Italian food filled every room. The dinner table was set with fresh, pressed white linens, white china, wine glasses and carafes. After they showed us to our rooms, Dave and I spent a few moments enjoying the surreal view of the Italian Alps from our balcony. Now time was moving too fast and I wanted everything to slow down.

Then the family began to arrive. Bianca and Carla came in first. I loved them the moment I saw them! Because we had spent the past year writing to each other, I felt like I already knew them so well. But nothing compared to meeting them face-to-face. Hearing their voices, touching them, hugging them, and looking into their eyes far exceeded my wildest dreams.

I could tell that Carla and Bianca loved life. They were very affectionate and loved to laugh. As we talked, we sat close together and often held hands. To my surprise, they both spoke English better than they led me to believe. A sisterly bonding began as we giggled and became acquainted through their broken English and my fractured Italian.

They loved Kate immediately and held her in their arms. Kate became the niece they had always dreamed of having. For about an hour, the three of us talked non-stop about our meeting for the first time by e-mail. We exchanged some tokens of love. I gave them jewelry that I had made for each of them. One of my hobbies was beading and I had a small collection of designs that I was eager to give them. Each piece was unique—just like them.

Then the phone rang. It was Viviana saying that she and her husband, Nico, were on their way. Bianca and Carla looked at each other with a raised eyebrow kind of grin. "What is it?" I asked. It was quite obvious that they had something that they wanted to share. "C'mon girls, is there something I need to know before Viviana arrives?" They were making me uneasy and a bit nervous.

They kept telling me that everything was fine and not to worry. I pressed them a little more. They said with a light laugh, "It might be better if you're not too forward and affectionate with Viviana at first. She will need time to warm up to you." I appreciated the warning more than they knew. I could see me running to Viviana and giving her a big bear hug that would shut her down or send her running.

The doorbell rang and Viviana and Nico walked in. I did my best to stay seated and give her time to take it all in. First, she greeted her papa and mama and then looked around. I could tell she was nervous and overwhelmed with the five new guests in the room. As she took off her jacket and found a place for her purse, she found her way to me. Slowly I stood to meet her. I reached for her extended hand and we greeted each other. I resisted giving her a hug. With the help of Bianca and Carla translating for us, we chatted a little.

As the other two sisters began talking to her, her tension eased. After a few minutes of small chat, I made my way around the room to talk to Papa Giulio and Jonas. From the corner of my eye, I saw Viviana watching me. I was deliberate about not being too affectionate with Papa Giulio or drawing any attention to myself. I tried to blend into the room and all of the family. The last thing in the world I wanted to do was to put up a wall between us or have her feel threatened by me. I knew she was feeling very protective of her father and was guarding her emotions.

The doorbell rang again. It was Giovanni and Stefano. Giovanni was Bianca's fiancé and Stefano was Carla's husband. They livened up the place with armfuls of wine and spirited enthusiasm. Dave and I warmed up to them right away. Stefano spoke fluent English. Giovanni spoke some, too, but he was a little rusty. I was so thankful that all of us could communicate and getting acquainted wasn't going to be as difficult as I once thought.

After all the greetings and introductions, Papa Giulio called us all around the table. Thirteen of us took our seats. Proudly, Giulio stood. Emotion poured out of him as he looked deeply into the eyes of all of his daughters. There were no more secrets, no more missing pieces, no more "what if's" to be played out. We were a family, together at last.

It was an international reunion like none other, with three languages being spoken (German, Italian, and English). Then out came a spread of food fit for royalty. Papa Giulio and Camile were in their glory as their guests marveled at every platter they laid before us. Bottles of wine were opened and as our glasses were filled, Papa Giulio gave the first toast *"alla mia cara famiglia!"* which means, "To my beloved family!"

And there we sat eating like kings with my new family in my father's small apartment in the mountain region of Italy. Until a year ago, I never even knew they existed and most of them didn't know I existed. This moment in time belonged to all of us, but there was something special between Papa Giulio and me. As I looked across the table, I could see the pride in his eyes. God's love was shining down on us that evening. God had been preparing us all for that day for many, many years.

Later that evening as Dave and I lay in bed, we relived the day. There was so much to take in and we had so much to share. We thanked God for every detail and every event that took place. It really was amazing to think that morning we were just beginning to make our way from Germany down

the long highway to Italy. We had been so wired with anticipation. We laughed about Uncle Jonas' entertainment in the
car with his singing and butchering songs—just to make me
laugh, and Sofia fussing at him to slow down and not drive
so fast. I remembered seeing Papa Giulio under the umbrella
and seeing his face for the first time. We quietly discussed
the photo album, the baby photo he had of me and how all
my doubts disappeared forever with that one little picture.
There had been so much to take in.

My mind was on sensory overload meeting my sisters and
their husbands. The food, the hospitality, the acceptance and
love were more than I could have ever asked or hoped for in a
lifetime. It was overwhelming! I couldn't have dreamed it. It
was a day I would never forget. And slowly, my weary mind
surrendered to rest—and I immediately began dreaming of
the next ten glorious days.

All Things New

The days that followed with Papa Giulio were an incredible time of renewal. We spent countless hours getting
acquainted. Each morning Papa met me with a warm embrace
and a kiss on the cheek that quickly made up for the years we
lost. He and Jonas had arranged for the entire family to spend
a week at a beach condo on the coast of Italy where our days
were filled playing together as a family on the beach and
taking casual strolls in Venice. We spent evenings around the
dinner table enjoying pasta, wine, and good conversations.
On one occasion, Papa Giulio took us to a restaurant he once
had owned. He looked so proud when one of the patrons
commented on our family resemblance. Reflecting back on
moments like those, I knew I had done the right thing.

By the third day of our reunion, Viviana warmed up to me
with a sweet genuine embrace. Following dinner that night,
she called me aside and conveyed to me her love and accep-

tance. Her distrust had vanished and every adverse feeling she had completely dissolved. From then on, as we'd gather around the dinner table, she would insist I sit in the seat next to Papa Giulio and she'd sit on his other side. Time flew by much too quickly as the days of our reunion came and went. In those moments together, I came to love each one of them deeply. To explain the deep sense of belonging that I felt would take pages and pages (and probably a doctorate in psychology). Suffice it to say, we became a bonded family. What some families never achieve in a lifetime, we accomplished in only ten days. It was intense and beautiful all at the same time.

Unfortunately, everything has an ending—at least temporarily. After ten days, our farewell ended like it began. With tears flowing and heartfelt emotions revealed, Uncle Jonas stood by my side and lovingly translated my final sentiments to each family member one by one, saving Papa Giulio for last. As my voice shook, the words struggled to get past the big lump of sadness in my throat. My eyes were drowning in tears and as I spoke words of love and gratitude to my papa, he held my face in his hands like when we first met ten days earlier. As we cried, he held me tightly in his arms. With his three daughters and Camile by his side, they watched and cried with him. I felt his thin frame tremble in my arms. He cried out, *"Andrea, Andrea, mi cara Andrea."*

"All The Days Ordained"

As I look back on this incredible reunion, I can't help but marvel at all the events that led up to it and all the people that had to cross my path in preparation for who I would become. I think of God's words in Psalms 139:16 declaring, "All the days ordained for me were written in your book before one of them came to be." Forever etched in my mind and imprinted on my heart, these memories, impressions and scenes were all part of His master plan including that most important talk with my mother at the beach, showing me that God's timing is impeccable. He waited until I was prepared. He orchestrated it so that all the key players were in place and seasoned enough to perform their parts. Then, as if His backstage work wasn't enough, He painted a golden sunset as a backdrop. My heavenly Father then pulled aside the curtain for me to hear those five words about my earthly father that would change my life, "He came back for you!"

Before you close this book, I want you to realize that Psalms 139 was written with you in mind, too. God has ordained your days as well. There are many people out there that have impacted your life, as you have affected others' lives, too, proving we are all part of a beautiful tapestry that God is weaving. And only God knows what it will look like it in the end.

Your tapestry may include making amends with someone who has hurt you deeply. It may involve *you* accepting responsibility for your past or it may mean leaving someone at the altar for God to take care of. One thing is for certain, God is in the business of restoring lives, not only spiritually, but in all areas of our lives. His love for us is not limited to eternal salvation alone, but for us to experience Him in an abundant life through forgiveness, mercy, compassion, healing and the kind of grace we don't deserve. So don't be afraid to look at the events of your life. Even the adversities have purpose. And in the end, you'll see God's magnificent handiwork and the amazing things He can do with an ordinary life like yours and mine.

Acknowledgments

Heavenly Father, You have lavished Your love and grace through the people You placed in my life.

Maureen Detmer and Maureen Haner, some of the sweetest days of this project were seeing you every week for our writing (and therapy) sessions! It was good for the soul. Your passion for writing and enthusiasm for living life well is what kept me going. Thank you for challenging me to dig deeper into the parts of my heart that I didn't know existed. You are both talented writers and equally gifted counselors. Thank you for sacrificing so much to work on this book.

To all my "test readers," that took the challenge to read a mess-of-a-manuscript and then gave me honest and encouraging feedback. Thank you for seeing the incredible story through the much needed re-writing and editing you sent me back to do.

Mom and Dad (Erika and Don), it is an honor to be your daughter. Thank you for your courage and being an example for me. You faced your fears, became a new creation, and then allowed Him to use the past to minister to others. That is a life well-lived!

Here's to my "cheering squad" that believed in me and helped nudge me off the cliff to write this book: Debra Burns, Kathe Krazeise, Fred and Jody Krazeise, Becky Storms, Laurie Wren, Monica Tichonoff, Lisa Caputo, Corin Hughs,

Jan Puterbaugh, Amy Joyce and my sister, Donna Galarza. Thanks also to my devoted staff and volunteers at the Sanford Crisis Pregnancy Center: Autha Lawlor, Linda McGrath, Jill Ankerson, Linda Wiehagen, Melynda Hani, Pam Bach, Karen Young, Debbie Yero, Dorothy Zeaton, Joanne Wit, Celines Martinez, Shirley Smith, Mim Mountford, Mindy Watton, and Suzie Carey. I love you all!

And of course, I am forever grateful to my dear husband, Dave, and our three children, David, Daniel, and Kate, for standing behind me and settling for a bowl of cereal when I would retreat for hours to write. You are the loves of my life and I await the glorious days ahead of us.

Author Contact:

If you would like to have **Andrea Krazeise** speak at your event, contact her at:
E-mail: andreak@cfl.rr.com
Website: www.andreakrazeise.com
Check out her website for a photo gallery of her family

About the Co-Authors:

Maureen Detmer works at the Sanford Crisis Pregnancy Center, serves on the Center's Board of Directors and is currently pursuing her passion for writing. Maureen and her husband live in Sanford and have two grown sons.

Maureen Haner has a doctorate in Christian education and another in Christian clinical counseling. She has worked with troubled teens and families for more than twenty-five years. In her spare time, she teaches music and pursues her passion to write.

Consider Getting Involved in Pro-Life Ministry:

If you have been inspired to be a part of the pro-life movement after reading this book, please consider supporting a Crisis Pregnancy Center in your area. If there is not a CPC in your area, please consider partnering with these ministries:

Sanford Crisis Pregnancy Center
Andrea Krazeise, Founder & Director
1002 French Ave.
Sanford, FL 32771
(407) 323-3384
Website: www.sanfordcpc.com
Email: sanfordcpc@netzero.net

Reveille Ministry, Inc.
Laurie Wren, Founder & Director
725 Primera Blvd. Suite #110
Lake Mary, FL 32746
(407) 333-0404
(866) 967-HOPE
Website: www.callforhope.org